'Once I made a dress in whose construction
100 yards of silk were employed.'

Charles Frederick Worth

Charles Frederick
Worth

The Englishman who invented Parisian *haute couture*

… with the invaluable help
of his French wife Marie
and the Empress Eugénie

STEPHEN CLARKE

MORE BOOKS BY STEPHEN CLARKE

Non-Fiction
1,000 Years of Annoying the French
Dirty Bertie, an English King Made in France
How the French Won Waterloo (or Think They Did)
The French Revolution & What Went Wrong
Talk to the Snail : the Ten Commandments for
  Understanding the French
Paris Revealed : the Secret Life of a City
Elizabeth II, Queen of Laughs

Château d'Hardelot, a Souvenir Guide
The British Invasion (with co-author Valli)
I Did It My Ways (with co-author D'yan Forest)
The Golden Treasure of the Entente Cordiale (chapter
  on Edward VII's diplomacy)

Fiction
A Year in the Merde
Merde Actually (US edition: In the Merde for Love)
Merde Happens
Dial M for Merde
The Merde Factor
Merde in Europe
A Brief History of the Future
Death Goes Viral (previously published as
  Who Killed Beano)
The Spy Who Inspired Me
Merde at the Paris Olympics

All material copyright © Stephen Clarke 2025

The moral right of Stephen Clarke to be identified as the author of this work has been asserted in accordance with the Copyright, Designs and Patents Act 1988.
All rights reserved.
No part of this publication may be reproduced, stored in a retrieval system or transmitted, in any form or by any means, electronic, mechanical, photocopying, recording or otherwise, without prior permission of the owner.

Cover design by Ruth Murray.
Large cover photos courtesy of Metmuseum.org.
Design assistance: Scott Clarke.

ISBN: 978-2-9585663-5-7

THANKS

The author is very grateful to members of the Worth family for their priceless help in overturning certain myths about their famous ancestors' life stories that had been repeated unchallenged in past biographies and articles.

Thanks especially to Olivia Worth van Hoegaerden for accompanying me to key places, for sharing family archives, for lending me valuable books, for introducing me to fruitful contacts, for giving me the family's version of supposedly well-known anecdotes, and for reading and commenting on my first draft. Merci beaucoup.

Thanks to Alexandra Worth for unveiling the family albums of press clippings and letters of condolence collected after Charles Frederick Worth's death.

Thanks to Paul Quincey, a descendant of Charles's maternal family, for sharing his research into the Worth family tree, for pointing me towards some excellent sources, and, again, for contradicting received wisdoms about Worth's start in life.

CONTENTS

	The Prologue	1
1	Provincial Beginnings	7
2	An Englishman in Paris	23
3	Revolution and Revival	33
4	A Traitor's Daughter	45
5	A Perfect Parisian Match	57
6	An Austrian Aid Package	73
7	The Worths Go to the Ball	81
8	The Birth of French *Haute Couture*	99
9	The Deadly Crinoline	119
10	The 'Little Hands' Who Made the Dresses	127
11	Things Can Only Get Better	139
12	A Palace of One's Own	159
13	Some People Don't Like the Cut of Worth's Cloth	167
14	The End of an Era	187
15	Anarchy in the City	199
16	Things Can Only Get Worse	207
17	New Beginnings	213
18	*Prêt à Porter*	225
19	Final Adjustments	235
	Epilogue	257
	Selective Bibliography	262

CHARLES FREDERICK WORTH

THE PROLOGUE

Just after dawn on a bright spring morning in 1860, a chic *Parisienne* called Valérie Feuillet began frantically knocking at a small window at number 7 rue de la Paix, a street near one of Paris's new boulevards.

She was on a desperate mission: that same evening, she was due to attend a banquet hosted by Eugénie, the wife of Emperor Napoléon III. A summons to dine at the Tuileries Palace was the most sought-after invitation in Paris, and Madame Feuillet needed a gown that would do justice to the glittering occasion. But the dress she had ordered from one of Paris's most renowned seamstresses, Madame Barenne, had arrived the day before, and it was a shocking disappointment. It was dowdy, unfashionable, unwearable. Valérie Feuillet knew that if she wore the gown, Eugénie was going to dismiss her as dull and ordinary, perhaps unworthy of a repeat invitation. Or, worse, the Empress would not even notice her. Madame Feuillet's only hope was to get up at dawn and drag another dressmaker – a man, this time – out of bed.

In Paris in 1860, male dressmakers were unheard of. Most chic French women created their wardrobes by buying fabric from a draper's shop, taking it to a *couturière* (female dressmaker) and instructing the woman to copy designs from a catalogue that might have been on the shelves for years. A renowned *couturière* like Madame Barenne would add a few extra adornments to the designs, but that was as far as her creativity went. She and her team of needle-workers would produce an expensive version of a tried and tested model.

In Madame Feuillet's case, this old method had failed. She now needed a miracle. And the man she wanted to haul out of bed had a growing reputation amongst a select group of *Parisiennes* as a miracle-worker – and as someone who might relish the chance to attract more publicity. His name was beginning to be whispered in the best houses in Paris – it was Worth. Yes, not only male, but English.

This Englishman did not work without female influence, of course. It was well known that his wife and model was also his publicist. Madame Worth was a frequent caller at the best bourgeois addresses in Paris, where she would bring samples of the most sumptuous fabrics and request an interview to show them to the mistress of the house. Wherever she went, Madame Worth would always be wearing one of her husband's innovative creations – which were, *bien sûr*, available in whichever fabric the client desired.

Madame Worth came from unsophisticated provincial stock – her voice still betrayed traces of an accent from her native Auvergne in central France, and she had an oval face with a strong jawline and dark eyebrows that was honest-looking rather than beautiful.

But she had learned poise and refined manners from decades of working for a Parisian draper, selling fabrics to the chic *dames* of the capital. Now she and her husband had opened a dress shop together, and her tireless campaigning was beginning to convince clients to call at the couple's new premises for a fitting.

On this particular morning Madame Feuillet was planning an unsolicited, out-of-hours visit there. From what she had heard about this English dressmaker, designing and producing a gown fit to dazzle the Empress Eugénie in only twelve hours would be his kind of challenge. Or so she hoped.

ღღღ

In her memoirs, Madame Feuillet describes the breathless suspense of that spring morning: she urges the half-asleep carriage driver to hurry across the awakening streets of Paris to the building with the polished brass plaque, Worth et Bobergh[1]. She taps on the window by the entrance and tugs on the bell rope until the concierge grudgingly opens the street door, allowing Madame F to rush upstairs, where she manages to convince a grumpy maid to take a scribbled begging letter to Monsieur and Madame Worth. She is careful to mention that her husband is Octave Feuillet, a writer very much in favour in imperial circles.

A few minutes later, a man emerges, 'still ruffled from the night', but draped in an elegant dressing gown. With his bushy moustache, high forehead and theatrical manner, he looks a little like an English cavalry lieutenant on leave. This is Charles Frederick Worth, former salesman in draper's shops, now co-owner of a Parisian dressmaking business.

Bizarrely, Monsieur Worth invites Madame Feuillet into his wife's bedroom, where she is still lying in her four-poster, swathed in a lacy nightgown. Madame

---

[1] Worth's associate, Otto Gustaf Bobergh, a Swedish cloth salesman, financed the new business. More about him later.

Feuillet apologizes for her intrusion, while Charles and Marie exchange meaningful glances.

'Alors Madame,' Charles Worth summarizes, in his wildly English accent, 'you require a gown for *this* evening? *Tonight?*'

'Oui, ce soir,' Madame Feuillet confirms.

The Worths look doubtful, almost mystified. Formal gowns are complex architectural affairs – there are pleats and folds, beading, usually several different fabrics, not to mention the crinoline, the bulky metal structure that holds the skirt of the dress out like an embroidered tent. A dress for that very evening? An absurd request.

'It would be an excellent opportunity to catch the Empress's eye,' Marie tells her husband. 'A challenge, too. A technical achievement,' she adds.

'If you succeed, your name will be on everyone's lips at the Palace,' Madame Feuillet says.

'*If* we succeed?' Suddenly Charles Worth is bounding around the room. 'It is an impossible task. But we can do it!'

'Your name and your graciousness have convinced us,' Marie adds. 'We will create your gown for the imperial banquet this evening.'

Charles is already striding towards the door.

Marie grips Madame Feuillet's hand. 'Inform your husband that you will be absent all day,' she tells the new client.

About twelve hours later, at the imperial palace, the dinner guests wait to be presented to their imperial hosts. Walking along the line, the Empress Eugénie stops in front of Valérie Feuillet and says: 'You must tell me the name of your *couturière*.'

'It is a man,' Valérie replies, 'and he is English.'

'Oh!' The Empress shows as much surprise as is

polite in Parisian high society. 'What do they call him?'

'Worth, Madame, and he has only recently opened a fashion house in Paris.'

The Empress nods approvingly. Valérie Feuillet's strategy has worked.

ʊʊʊ

The Empress Eugénie was not the only person in Paris to be surprised, shocked even, that a man should be making dresses. The entry for *'couturier'* (male dressmaker) in the Larousse French encyclopedia, published a few years later, contains a long diatribe against this crossing of sexual boundaries, which starts: 'We are now seeing the indescribable peculiarity of men (are they really men?) presiding over the outfitting of women.'

In fact the writer, Pierre Larousse, was forgetting that Worth was not Paris's first male dressmaker in living memory. Napoléon Bonaparte's first wife, Joséphine, had her coronation dress made by a man, Louis Hippolyte Le Roy. However, Le Roy hadn't actually *designed* the dress. He had only supervised its manufacture. He had been less a dressmaker than the manager of a team of seamstresses.

Even so, the subtext in Larousse's encyclopaedia was clear – if a man like Charles Worth was making dresses, he had to be gay. Or, more to the point, he *had better be gay*, otherwise some very macho French husbands were going to be knocking at his door, demanding more than a dress fitting. Duels were common at the time, and meddlers like Worth often ended up taking a dawn carriage ride to the Bois de Boulogne, to receive a pistol bullet in the chest.

The outrage about male dressmaking went even deeper: not long after Valérie Feuillet's social triumph, it was being whispered in Paris that Charles Worth was the only man allowed to see the Empress Eugénie in her *négligée* – a sight long since denied to her own husband, Napoléon III. Was it possible that a common Englishman (and Worth was definitely both of those things) was cuckolding the Emperor of France?

Well, no, almost certainly not, because Charles was happily married to his soulmate. In any case he did not attend fittings when his clients were in their underwear – only Marie and female seamstresses were present before the lady was decent, and wearing the initial version of the dress that was being made for her.

But from the first meeting between Charles Worth and the Empress Eugénie in the spring of 1860, they would form a duo that was going to scandalize France, make both their names world-famous, and create a whole new industry – French *haute couture*.

At first sight, they had almost nothing in common. Eugénie, born a Spanish countess, was married to an emperor, while Charles had survived Dickensian hardship in Lincolnshire and London to become a glorified shopkeeper, and was in business alongside his wife Marie, whose origins were as humble as his.

But the three of them shared traits that can unite the most unlikely co-conspirators: an almost religious love of beautiful things; a sense that they were outsiders in snobbish Paris; and, perhaps most importantly, a burning ambition to prove themselves.

For the last four decades of the 19th century – probably France's most creative, vibrant period – this melding of minds and intentions was going to make the Worths invincible.

1 PROVINCIAL BEGINNINGS

Charles and Marie Worth were products of the social mobility that the 19th century offered to people with talent and ambition.

To give a few famous examples: Charles Dickens started life as a child worker in a shoe-polish factory. Marie Curie was a penniless Polish immigrant when she first began assisting in the Parisian laboratory where she would later discover radium. Isaac Singer was scraping a living in Boston when he was asked to repair a cumbersome sewing machine; days later, he had built a prototype that would turn him into one of America's richest industrialists.

The 19th century is peppered with similar success stories. Charles Frederick Worth's life is exceptional in that it combined *all* the above elements. He started out as a Dickensian child apprentice; then, like Marie Curie, he arrived penniless in Paris; like Isaac Singer, he more or less invented a new industry. And like all three of them, he did it using his inner resources of creativity, hard-earned skill, and a very Victorian – and Napoleonic – eye for an opportunity.

In all of this, Worth was urged on and actively aided by his colleague, and later wife, Marie, née Vernet.

Marie Worth's role in this success story is often understated. She was not merely the woman *behind* the famous man – she was always *beside* Charles, from his first attempts at designing dresses to the launch of the brand that would make Worth the most famous fashion name in 19th-century Europe.

In some ways, she was *in front of* him, as the public face (and body) of his style. It was by wearing his designs to work that Marie would win over his earliest clients.

Marie arrived in Paris and began working there in the textile industry several years before her future husband. She was an apprentice and then sales assistant in the same fabric shop where Charles would later apply for a job. So let's look at her background first.

ϖϖϖ

Marie Augustine Vernet was born in the centre of Clermont-Ferrand on 26 August 1825, the second daughter of a tax collector.

Clermont-Ferrand would later expand into the home of the Michelin tyre manufacturers (a first rubber factory was set up there in 1832), but in the 1820s it was the centre of a cereal-producing region, and had recently become known for its pasta and semolina. Genoese and Piedmontese soldiers, demobilized from Bonaparte's army when he was toppled in 1815, had come to Clermont-Ferrand and created a noodle industry using the local wheat.

Marie's parents devoted a lot of effort to marrying off their elder daughter, Irma, and even offered prospective suitors a dowry. Irma was an attractive girl, and managed to marry 'well', to an architect called Denis Darcy, who was working in Paris as part of the team renovating Notre-Dame cathedral[2].

As the second daughter, young Marie's prospects were much less promising, especially when her father was demoted to a mere office clerk, perhaps (and this is pure guesswork) for adding people's taxes into his own personal collection. Before the French Revolution, that was how royal tax collectors had made their living. In any case, there was no money for a dowry for Marie, and all Clermont-Ferrand had to offer her was a future in either farming or fettuccine.

Her mother decided to put all her eggs into the Parisian basket. Madame Vernet seems to have left her husband after his demotion, perhaps because of the public disgrace. Before Irma's wedding, she took both her daughters to the capital, where they found lodgings in the rue Saint Marc, a kilometre north of the Louvre. This was the garment district, so it was only logical that Marie, the provincial teenager without a fiancé, should be sent to work in the neighbourhood's textile industry.

Marie's son Jean-Philippe Worth describes her upbringing in his family history, *A Century of Fashion*[3].

---

[2] This was the phase of work on the cathedral that would end in 1859 with the addition of the new spire that so spectacularly burned down in 2019.

[3] Jean-Philippe Worth's book is credited as being written by him and translated by an American journalist and author called Ruth Scott Miller. In her foreword to the book, she says that she met Jean-Philippe at his home. According to the Worth family today, at least parts of her interviews were probably conducted in English, which Jean-Philippe spoke fluently. He died in 1926, without re-reading the manuscript, which was published in 1928. It does not seem to have been published in its original French version. The book can therefore be unreliable. This was a time when interviews were not recorded, so everything Jean-Philippe

Her education was, he says, 'summary. She was taught gracefulness and how to walk and how to dance. To this was added some spelling, addition, subtraction, division and multiplication, a little of geography and sewing.'

Girls of middle-class stock, cash-poor but well turned-out and semi-educated, were exactly what the Paris's fabric sellers were looking for, and Marie was taken on as an apprentice salesgirl at the capital's most famous draper's shop, La Maison Gagelin, at 93 rue de Richelieu[4].

ღღღ

The rue de Richelieu was one of the city centre's wider and more salubrious medieval streets, and the main thoroughfare of the garment district. Just down the road, in a line, stood three of Gagelin's direct competitors: Au Persan, La Compagnie des Indes, and Rosset et Normand. Chic women from all over France came here in search of the best-quality fabrics to take to their dressmakers. Merchandise listed on La Maison Gagelin's bills included 'silks, Indian and French cashmeres, [...] gold and silver embroideries, French and foreign fancy fabrics, painted muslins, poplins, fine Merino wools, [...]

---

said to Ruth Scott Miller was transcribed from her notes, and we cannot be entirely sure what she noted and what she added. She may have misinterpreted things said in French. What was more, Jean-Philippe was sometimes recalling stories told to him by his parents, whose memories were not perfect. Despite all this, in general the book is an invaluable source of information.

[4] Incidentally, the first-ever French croissants were baked almost opposite, at 92 rue de Richelieu, in the Boulangerie Viennoise founded in 1840 by a former Austrian soldier called August Zang.

mourning fabrics, [...] veils, scarves and frills at makers' prices.'

All these cloth merchants were conveniently located near the workshops of Paris's best-known dressmakers. At number 102 rue de Richelieu, for example, directly opposite La Maison Gagelin, were the premises of Madame Delatour, outfitter to King Louis-Philippe's wife, Queen Marie-Amélie. Just down the street from Gagelin, at number 89, was a shop that had previously belonged to Joséphine Bonaparte's stylist, Louis Hippolyte Le Roy. In April 1789, just before the July Revolution, another royal dressmaker, Mademoiselle Bertin, had moved in at number 26, and stayed there until her death in 1813, having survived several regime changes. In Paris, fashion outlasts politicians. As if to prove this point, Gagelin had a drawing on the wall of one of its main reception rooms of Marie-Antoinette coming to shop there shortly after her arrival in Paris.

ϖϖϖ

La Maison Gagelin was a business run for and by women. Founded in the 1830s by Charles Louis Gagelin, since 1839 it had been co-owned[5] by his wife Marie Élisabeth and their son-in law, Octave Opigez, the husband of their daughter Marie Aglaé Gagelin. It had kept the Gagelin name because its reputation was based on Marie Aglaé's good taste and intuition. She bought the fabrics while her husband took care of the admin and her mother acted as a sort of hostess, greeting customers.

---

[5] At this time it was illegal for married women to be sole legal owners of a business in France until 1907. And until 1965 French wives were still not able to open their own bank account without their husband's consent; by law, men managed the family finances.

It sounds like a female-friendly working environment for the young Marie Vernet, but the Mesdames Gagelin were no fairy godmothers.

Like any trainee salesgirl in Paris, Marie worked for no wages. On the contrary, at the time, parents would usually have to pay the employer for a salesgirl's apprenticeship.

Marie Vernet was sixteen, so she was legally an adult, and could work twelve hours a day, seven days a week. A statutory day off for workers was not granted in France until 1906.

Younger apprentices were treated little better. In 1841, a law was passed in France setting the minimum working age at eight. Until children were twelve, they could work eight hours a day, six days a week. From ages twelve to sixteen, the working day was twelve hours. After sixteen, the employer's word was law.

Once Marie became an acceptable *demoiselle de magasin* (literally a 'shop miss', though it sounds much fancier in French) she received a small wage, but not enough to branch out and live independently.

In short, working in a fashionable draper's shop at the heart of Paris was, like many 19th-century jobs in the service sector, a well-dressed form of slavery. For most women, the only respectable way to escape was marriage – with the hope that the husband would be sober and solvent.

ʊʊʊ

On the other side of the Channel, Charles Frederick Worth was born a few weeks after Marie Vernet, on 13 October 1825.

He was his parents' fifth child, but he had only two

surviving siblings, an older brother and sister.[6]

The Worths were more privileged than the Vernets – Charles Frederick was the son of a solicitor in the agricultural town of Bourne, Lincolnshire. The boy started life learning to read, write and behave like a gentleman, being groomed to become a member of the solid, well-off middle class.

In 1825, Bourne was a more dynamic version of Clermont-Ferrand. A major centre for grain milling and dealing, it was an important stop on the north-south route from Lincoln to London. Charles's father, William Worth II, was well established there, and the family initially lived in a large, three-storey home, Wake House, a prominent building on the main road into the town centre.

Charles might well have completed his education and gone into the legal profession. But his father was a drinker who fell into the habit of losing heavily on horseracing, bare-knuckle boxing matches and cockfights – any event where bets were being laid. According to the Worth family today, this recklessness may well have been due to bi-polarity, which was of course undiagnosed at the time. It is also rumoured that William caught syphilis from a prostitute, which caused his mental decline.

In any case, when Charles was eleven, William Worth

---

[6] Two other children had died in infancy, one of them in 1824 – a boy who had been baptised Charles. The disappointment of this loss was apparently so great that when, very soon afterwards, another son was born, his parents named him Charles Frederick. The family considered (and some members still consider) Charles Frederick his true first name, a double-barrelled French-style title, like Jean-Philippe or Marie-Claude. In this book, however, to save reading time, he will usually be referred to simply as Charles. Apologies for this serial inaccuracy.

II went bankrupt and abandoned the family, leaving his wife Ann to fend for herself and her younger son: Charles's elder brother had already left home and gone to work for HM Customs, while his sister had recently died.

Ann Worth, née Quincey, came from a fairly wealthy background, but according to most of Charles's past biographers, there was little solidarity between family members, and she was forced to become the unpaid, live-in housekeeper to her own relations – a humiliating comedown.

However, a current member of the family, Paul Quincey, points out that Ann had two widowed sisters living nearby, and that is it most likely that she moved in with one of them, not as a housekeeper but as a relative who had fallen on hard times. Naturally, Ann would have helped out with the housework, and would not have expected a salary. In the early 1800s, there were many widowed or unmarried siblings living together, keeping up middle-class appearances on their meagre but sufficient incomes.

Even so, one thing is certain: times were suddenly hard enough for young Charles to be taken out of school and sent to work for a printer.

The Brits were a few years ahead of France with their child employment laws, but working conditions were just as harsh. The Cotton Mills Regulation Act of 1825 ensured that children aged between nine and sixteen would work a twelve-hour day from Monday to Friday, plus nine hours on Saturday. And this was announced as progress, because before that, child working hours had been limitless. To re-assure employers, a mill-owning MP supported the bill with a speech promising that children would work 'with greater vigour and activity' during their reduced hours.

ʊʊʊ

It was now that the young Charles Worth had his first Dickensian moment: here was a boy who had spent his weekdays in schoolbooks and his free time at play, but who was now obliged to endure dirty manual labour, with no time to do anything that stimulated his mind. So after a year of this ordeal, he begged his mother to let him leave the printing works. He didn't mind working hard, he said, but if he stayed there, he was afraid he was going to die – whether of exhaustion, boredom or ink poisoning, it is not clear.

In later life, he confessed to having 'an instinctive repugnance to soiling my fingers,' though this sounds as though he was making very light of a tough and dirty apprenticeship.

Charles had been a live-in apprentice at the printer's, sleeping on the workshop floor, so he needed to find another job with accommodation. And at the age of only twelve, he already knew what he wanted to do. The boy Charles told his mother, 'I'm not learning anything, not getting anywhere. I never was intended to be a printer. Please let me leave it and go to London, go into some shop, any place where I'll have a chance.'

Charles's family already had connections in the clothing industry on his father's side. His paternal grandmother was the daughter of a village tailor, and an uncle (his father's sister's husband) was a draper in the small Lincolnshire town of Horbling[7]. Perhaps this gave young Charles the idea of working with fabrics.

---

[7] Also the town where Charles's parents were married.

However, he seems to have set his sights much higher than Lincolnshire. In some autobiographical notes published in March 1895 in an American newspaper, the *Union and Advertiser*, in Rochester, New York State, Charles wrote that he had always dreamt of going to live in London and: 'Chancing to know a gentleman who was then a solicitor on Parliament Street I wrote to him begging him to find some position for me in the capital.' In reality, though, it seems more likely that it was his relatives in the textile trade who pulled a few strings and found him a job with Swan & Edgar, a fashionable draper's shop in central London.

In the early spring of 1838, mother and son raised some money decorating Easter bonnets, and Ann accompanied Charles on the coach to London where he was to start his apprenticeship.

ʊʊʊ

Within a few years, Swan & Edgar would expand into a large department store taking up a whole section of Piccadilly Circus, but when Worth joined the business, it was still relatively small, located in elegant, balcony-fronted premises at 49 Regent Street. One of the founders, George Swan, had died, and the shop was now run by William Edgar who, it was said, as a young man walked to London from his native Carlisle (a distance of 420 kilometres), and taken a job as a market trader selling haberdashery. The story was that, having nowhere to stay, he used to sleep under his stall in Haymarket every night, until he found a business partner, George Swan, and opened a shop.

Perhaps these humble beginnings helped William Edgar to create the kind of working environment in which a young apprentice like Charles Worth, fresh in from the sticks, could start to enjoy life. Charles was unpaid and lived in an all-male dormitory on the premises, but he relished the chance to learn all about the textile trade.

His days of ink and oily printing presses were over. Now his universe was hung with silk and velvet[8], displayed in shimmering rolls of every imaginable hue. We often imagine the 19th century in black and white, but the Victorians went in for a whole paintbox of colours, with bold shades of green, purple, pink and blue that they used with abandon. For twelve hours a day, Charles memorized the names of different types of material, he learned to recognize the patterns woven into ribbons and brocades, and the different styles and origins of lace. He handled elegant shawls and even hosiery – the undergarments that decorated ladies' (hidden) legs.

The Lincolnshire lad also got to frequent, or at least observe, some of London's chicest women. William Edgar made a point of being in the store personally to serve his most important customers, including the young Queen Victoria. But on any normal day, the shop was brimming with regal ladies and their fine hats, lacy parasols and supercilious expressions. At Swan & Edgar's, these *grandes dames* would temporarily put themselves into a position of subservience to their social inferiors, listening to advice and accepting suggestions from mere salespeople.

All this was ammunition for the future career of Charles Frederick Worth, who was learning the rag trade from the raw materials upwards, and who would later

---

[8] Swan & Edgar also sold less glamorous materials like sealskin, but we will not dwell on those.

make a name for himself bossing these very same ladies about, ordering them to wear the fabrics that he selected for them.

☙☙☙

During his seven-year apprenticeship in London, Worth matured into a tall, well-spoken, elegant youth, and a confident salesman. His older colleagues showed him how to become a dandy without spending a fortune.

Using money from delivery tips, he bought smart, well-cut clothes at staff discount prices from Swan & Edgar's men's department. There is a drawing of the 14-year-old Charles, no doubt sketched for a few pennies by a pavement artist, that shows him wearing a stiff collar, rakish bow tie, natty jacket and waistcoat, his hair neatly parted, his face a model of calm self-confidence. In a couple of years he had come a very long way from the rustic, ink-splashed printer's apprentice.

Charles also educated himself in art and aesthetics. He had very little spending money, so he couldn't go to the theatre or the pub. Instead, he spent rare days off admiring the paintings at the Dulwich Picture Gallery and the newly opened National Gallery – neither of which charged an entrance fee.

The National Gallery was small but contained masterpieces by Van Dyck, Titian and Gainsborough, all of whom painted sumptuous fabrics in their portraits.

Worth was especially impressed by a portrait of Queen Elizabeth I in all her jewel-encrusted glory, wearing a wide, tight-waisted dress that could well be an inspiration for the tent-like crinolines that Charles would later play a major part in popularizing – and then doing away with once they had become too bulky.[9]

What is now trendy Soho was a slum area in the early 1840s, but if the young Worth wandered westwards from Regent Street, he was in the residential districts of Piccadilly, St James and Mayfair, where he saw the cream of London society, either parading in open carriages or strolling. The promenaders might well have included Louis-Napoléon Bonaparte, the future Emperor Napoléon III of France, who was in political exile in England and living in Carlton House Terrace, not far from Trafalgar Square and Nelson's Column.[10] The Frenchman would often strut along Regent Street, drawn there by the men's tailors in the neighbourhood and, perhaps, the number of women out shopping.

And Louis-Napoléon wasn't alone – all the dandies of London would be there, showing off their trim figures in waist-hugging jackets, wide-collared waistcoats and crisp linen shirts. The dandy-in-chief at the time was another Frenchman in exile, a friend and supporter of Louis-Napoléon called Alfred d'Orsay. He had married a rich English heiress and now spent his days at social events, delighting guests with his ever-changing outfits. His evenings were probably given over to more louche pursuits in the men's clubs around Regent Street.

In later life, Worth said that he noticed how these London gentlemen renewed their wardrobe constantly, whereas many of Swan & Edgar's female clients chose their dress fabric simply because it was long-lasting, and had it made up into designs that rarely evolved. When

---

[9] The crinoline, that absurd, often dangerous, female fashion will be discussed at length in Chapter 9.
[10] It can't have been pleasant for this proud nephew of Napoléon Bonaparte to be living in the shadow of the English sailor who smashed the French fleet in 1805.

English women weren't at a special occasion, they would usually wear plain dresses, enlivened only by an elaborate shawl, and would hide their faces under the brim of a bonnet.

Worth probably read about fashion in the *Illustrated London News*, a popular weekly paper that published reports on world events, accompanied, as its name suggests, by illustrations. The newspaper cost sixpence, which was beyond the means of an unpaid apprentice, but Charles would have been able to peruse old copies at the shop. Most of the articles and engravings dealt with battles, storms, riots and disasters, but they also depicted Queen Victoria's dresses when she attended processions or balls.

ӧӧӧ

Worth's attention was certainly attracted towards all things French in 1843, when it was reported in the British press that Queen Victoria was to make a state visit to King Louis-Philippe's France (marking the first thaw in Anglo-French relations since the Napoleonic Wars). The papers mentioned that for the state visit, the Queen acquired dresses from a Parisian designer called Madame Camille. She was renowned as an adventurous designer. A French newspaper, the *Revue de Paris,* said of Madame Camille that she took inspiration from 'Greek bodices, Turkish sleeves, Polish jackets, Chinese tunics. Everything inspires her, and out of all these foreign clothes she makes French dresses. It is bizarre, audacious, but always pretty.'[11]

The English newspapers reported Victoria arriving in France in September 1843 wearing purple satin with a

---

[11] From an article published in the *Revue de Paris* in January 1847.

yellow feathered bonnet, followed on her first evening by a dress of crimson velvet and a diamond headdress, and next day, a 'tartan dress with black mantle, or pelerine[12], and yellow drawn silk bonnet.' Madame Camille clearly had eclectic tastes.

As the royal couple set off, the young Charles Frederick Worth went to watch Victoria and Albert riding along the Mall on their way to catch the steamer to Normandy. Perhaps he began to think then: if they can visit France, why can't I?

With a little less luggage, perhaps.

---

[12] A small cape that covered the shoulders.

2 AN ENGLISHMAN IN PARIS

By 1845, Charles Frederick Worth's evolution into an expert fabric salesman was complete. Not yet 20, he had created a fully-fledged persona for himself, and now looked every bit the London gentleman. Only the traces of his Lincolnshire burr and his lack of gold watch and signet ring betrayed his modest background. His apprenticeship over, he needed to move on.

Here again, Worth's memories in later life seem to be too streamlined to be accurate. In the reminiscences published in the Rochester *Union and Advertiser*, he recalled that:

> I was wont in those days to talk a great deal to the buyers, who were sent from London to Paris, about matters and things in the latter city. A visit to Paris was then no small undertaking. The actual journey took two days and a half each way, so that the buyers from the house of Swan & Edgar used to consume from sixteen to seventeen days for each visit. Finally, Paris became the goal of my aspirations, as London had formerly been. I used to spend my evenings in the study of French, and whenever any French customers visited the shop I invariably

sought them out and tried my best to talk with them.

One of my customers went into business at Caen, and I was in hopes that he would take me into partnership; but, on being disappointed in that quarter I resolved upon going to Paris and trying my fortune there at all hazards. I had no idea of where I should go or what I should do when I got there. But I was so fortunate as to obtain a position almost immediately in the house of Messrs Gagelin & Co. in the Rue Richelieu, then one of the most extensive and best-known establishments of its kind in Paris.

In reality, the transition from Swan & Edgar to Paris was probably not so smooth. It is possible that before leaving for France, Charles became a salesman with an even more prestigious London silk merchant, Lewis & Allenby, also in Regent Street. But it seems to be true that the idea of patiently building a London career in a shop did not appeal to him. France was calling, so he asked his mother to help him make the pilgrimage across the Channel to Paris, the capital of fashion.

At that time, Charles probably thought that a few years working in France would enable him to return to England and land a well-paid post as a buyer for one of the big fabric merchants. Either Swan & Edgar or Lewis & Allenby must have approved the idea, because Charles would not have considered moving on without a glowing reference in his pocket.

He needed cash to finance his self-improvement scheme. The story usually told is that he turned to his mother, and that the more or less penniless Worth *Mère* went cap in hand to her family who advanced their ambitious young relative five pounds (about £1,500 in modern money) to finance his trip.

However, Paul Quincey thinks this unlikely. In his opinion, Charles's mother would not have countenanced a move to a country that in many English minds was still the enemy – one of Charles's uncles had actually fought at Waterloo 30 years earlier. What was more, she would have been horrified to see the fresh-faced shop assistant, barely out of his teens, venturing into completely uncharted territory, with no family, friends or contacts to bail him out if things went wrong. Paul therefore thinks that Charles defied his mother, who had spent years suffering the consequences of her drunken husband's failed get-rich-quick schemes and, if she did give her assent, she would have advised her son to save up some money first, or wait for his employers to offer him a posting. In Paul Quincey's words: 'No doubt [Charles] went to Paris both with a strong determination to prove his family wrong – which he did – and to support his mother financially – which, sadly, her early death in 1852 made impossible.'

One thing we know for sure: the young Charles begged, saved and borrowed five pounds, plus enough to buy himself a ticket on the steamer from London Bridge to Boulogne-sur-Mer, followed by a cheap outdoor seat on the stagecoach to Paris. This was a 25-hour journey across northern France that would have tested the most ambitious traveller's resolve.

Luckily, it was late spring or early summer, so Charles arrived in Paris without contracting pneumonia. But, his joints stiff, he jumped down from the coach to begin his new life with only his carpet bag of meagre possessions and the five pounds in his pocket. Nowhere to live, no job – and little or no French except what he had learned back in London.

ϖϖϖ

Paris must have come as a shock to a young man fed on newspaper descriptions of state visits and satin dresses. Only a few of the new, airy boulevards had been opened up, so most of the city centre was a malodorous maze of cobbled medieval streets. Everywhere there was filth underfoot and the place was, of course, packed with Parisians, who have never been the most welcoming and easy-going of city folk.

Outside the chic residential neighbourhoods of western Paris, the people thronging the streets were poor – the kind who, given the slightest provocation, would erect barricades, storm palaces, and do their best to rob and/or decapitate as many of their social superiors as possible before soldiers marched in to restore order or join in the rioting, depending on which way the political pendulum was swinging.

So it is admirable that the young Englishman Charles Worth, who had until recently been living above a smart Regent Street silk merchant's shop with all meals provided, quickly found himself a Parisian garret room.

He also got a job. Or jobs. In his account in the Rochester newspaper, he glossed over this period, but it is likely that he initially had several goes at menial work, to improve his French and eke out his savings. Eventually, no doubt after several months, he was taken on at a draper's shop called La Ville de Paris, where he swept up and sold six days a week, from eight in the morning until eight at night, before going back to his room to study French by candlelight.

He had arrived in the Parisian textile industry, albeit on one of the lowest rungs.

ʊʊʊ

It was probably after more than a year of this apprenticeship in being Parisian that Charles was finally ready to take his first step up the French ladder. And it was a daunting one. Having now learnt all the French vocabulary of his trade – colours, fabrics, textures, as well as the salesman's patter – he went to apply for a post at one of Paris's most renowned drapers.

This was La Maison Gagelin, where a certain Marie Vernet was working.

Its quiet luxuriousness must have brought back reassuring memories of Swan & Edgar. Its floors were covered in Persian rugs, there were crystal chandeliers, gilded armchairs, and mirrors hung with lush fabrics. Smartly dressed assistants loitered politely. It looked like the lounge of a five-star hotel. Only the mahogany counters, wide enough to unfurl rolls of fabric, gave the premises' real vocation away.

There were no dresses on show, just a few carefully-draped shawls, cloaks and fabric samples.

This was an atmosphere designed to inspire reverence in the haughtiest client, but Worth would not have felt intimidated. He had applied to Gagelin's once before, shortly after he arrived in Paris, and been rejected because of his atrocious French. But now he knew both its language and its techniques.

He was escorted into an office where he explained why an English sales assistant would be an asset to La Maison Gagelin: since the exchange of state visits between King Louis-Philippe and Queen Victoria in 1843, Anglo-French relations were cordial. English tourists were trooping into Paris and – then as now – not all of them were capable of speaking French or trusting foreign salesmen. Charles would be able to sell to them in their own language.

It was an excellent argument. The rue de Richelieu was a street where the whole of Europe came to shop. Madame Delatour, for example, at number 102, listed herself as 'by appointment to foreign courts'. Her use of the plural implied how much currency was to be earned.

In general, a command of English was seen as a positive amongst the French: Louis-Philippe's ability to speak to Victoria in her native language had been noted in the French press, causing, according to one journalist, 'a furious jealousy in Monsieur Guizot', the prime minister.

What was more, Charles told his prospective employers, native Parisians even seemed to enjoy his English accent when he spoke French. Madame Gagelin and Monsieur Opigez would have nodded at this. Whereas British people find a French person speaking English inherently comic or lascivious, the French are convinced that any Brit who can master French pronunciation must be a lord or a lady.

And Charles, a tall, tastefully dressed young man with dark, piercing eyes and a good-natured face, made an excellent first impression, even if his clothes were too worn to make him look rich.

He was told that, if he joined the staff at La Maison Gagelin, he would have to buy a new outfit from the shop, so that he would always be perfectly turned out. The cost of work clothes was deducted in weekly instalments from employees' pay. To this, Charles readily acceded. He had done the same at Swan & Edgar, and always saw clothing as a wise investment.

After an interview lasting barely a quarter of an hour, Charles was hired. And he immediately began to make an impact. His main job was to recommend fabrics and sing the praises of ready-made shawls, wraps and cloaks. Gagelin's fussy clients would often give staff the runaround, demanding that endless rolls of cloth should be fetched, or wraps unwrapped. One of the sales techniques that Charles imported from London worked especially well in such cases.

When he had a difficult customer – looking for a shawl, for example – Charles would let the client reject every item he suggested. Then, resignedly, he would confess that he had 'a marvellous shawl, of superb craftmanship, but I'm not sure you would be willing to pay that much.' The client would demand to see it immediately, so Worth would fetch one of the first shawls he had suggested, and drape it over the shoulders of a salesgirl, 'with a gesture of reverence and triumph'[13].

Nine out of ten times, the ruse worked. Charles found that it was far easier to sell a shawl or scarf when it was being worn, especially if the buyer was an indecisive man. If a salesgirl put it on and did a twirl, a male customer could judge for himself how it would look on his wife or loved one.

Soon after starting his new job, Charles's was paired with the ideal model for this strategy: Marie Vernet. She had a natural elegance, a friendly face that inspired confidence, and attractive eyes of sapphire blue. She made everything she wore look just right.

By the time Charles arrived at the shop, Marie had

---

[13] According to Jean-Philippe Worth.

graduated to earning a small salary in exchange for her twelve-hour day as a *demoiselle de magasin*.

Initially, the deference she had been trained in, and her own shyness in the face of snobbish eyes, made her uncomfortable in this modelling role, but she quickly recognized that her new colleague produced results. The tall, polite Englishman and the dark-haired, blue-eyed *Auvergnate* formed a formidable team.

But selling shawls, even with the novelty of doing so in French, did not satisfy Charles for long. He had other ambitions. He had noted that, just as in London, French dressmakers did not actually *design* garments, and fabric shops did not sell clothes, apart from their ready-made accessories such as the scarves and shawls.

An immense order soon after Charles's arrival at the Maison Gagelin underlined this demarcation between trades. In the early autumn of 1846, it was announced that there would be a double wedding in the Spanish royal family. Queen Isabel, who was only 16, urgently needed a husband, and had settled on a 24-year-old cousin called Francisco – who was openly homosexual.

Meanwhile, the King of France, Louis-Philippe, had convinced Queen Isabel that his own son should marry her younger sister, the 14-year-old Princess María Louisa Fernanda, on the same day. That way, if Isabel and her gay husband did not have any children, María Louisa Fernanda's half-French offspring would be in line to inherit the throne of Spain.[14]

The upshot of this Franco-Spanish wrangling was that

---

[14] In the event, Isabel and Francisco had eleven children, all of them fathered by Isabel's lovers. Francisco did not mind this in the least, apparently, and even named his dogs after the lovers in question.

a huge number of dresses had to be made in a very short time for the double wedding – for the brides and their attendants, both for the ceremony itself and all the ensuing celebrations. And, naturally enough, the dresses were ordered from fashionable Paris.

Queen Isabel's own wardrobe was commissioned from the famous Madame Camille, who had to produce 52 dresses in about two weeks. The actual wedding dress was not a problem. A dressmaker like Madame Camille always had a white *pièce de résistance* in her workshop that just needed customizing for any client who was rich enough to buy it. In Isabel's case, this mainly involved letting out the seams to fit her more-than-ample figure.

For the remaining 51 gowns, Madame Camille put in a bulk order for fabrics and trimmings with La Maison Gagelin. Charles Worth, who had been forming his own ideas about design ever since he walked the streets of London and leafed through the *Illustrated London News*, must have found it frustrating to see the rolls of cloth and packages of buttons and brocades disappear out of his reach, into workshops just a few doors away.

He would later confess that he quickly began to feel that Parisian women were disappointing, in their fashion sense at least. They were no more inventively dressed than Londoners, and ladies would always use a shawl or cloak to liven up dresses that varied little in pattern and were often too fussily adorned with frills. Paris's dressmakers, he felt, were resting on their laurels. The famous *couturières* like Madame Camille were ready to be knocked off their pedestal.

3 REVOLUTION AND REVIVAL

For the moment, the only person to be toppled was King Louis-Philippe. In February 1848, Paris organized another of its revolutions. The King and his family fled into exile to England, while their palace, the Tuileries – just down the road from La Maison Gagelin – was ransacked, and fierce street fighting broke out across the city.

Fortunately, the violence was relatively short-lived compared to 1789, albeit brutal. After a few days of barricades, mass arrests of protesters and some massacres by the army causing around 6,500 deaths, a new republic was announced. Its first president was that former *habitué* of Regent Street, the dandy Louis-Napoléon Bonaparte. He had returned from exile in England, flouting a French law that banned members of former ruling families from entering the country, and stood in an election that saw him win 72% of the vote.

This victory surprised many members of France's political establishment. Until then, Louis-Napoléon had been regarded as something of a clown, repeatedly tripping over while trying to follow in his famous uncle's footsteps. Twice he had mounted absurd attempts at a repeat of 1814, when the first *Empereur* had escaped from captivity on the island of Elba, landed with his personal guards in Cannes and rounded up an army of followers as he marched towards Paris. Emulating this triumph, Louis-Napoléon had arrived in Strasbourg in 1836 and Boulogne-sur-Mer in 1840, hoping to win over the local regiments before storming the capital. Both times he had failed miserably, getting exiled to America the first time and imprisoned for six years the second.

By 1848, though, he had learned his lesson and used more modern methods, publishing pamphlets that set out his plan to return France to Napoleonic glory (a sort of 'Make France Great Again' campaign). Now, to the astonishment of France's many anti-Bonapartists, and even to some of his own family, the former clown was in power, and legitimately.

ღღღ

However, any revolution, peaceful or not, hits the pockets of traders in non-essential goods. During periods of political upheaval, people naturally spend their money on daily survival. In Paris in early 1848, buying a cashmere shawl or ordering a new silk dress became a dispensable luxury. Meanwhile, the big money flowed out of the city in the pockets of royalists, while foreign tourists deleted France from their must-see list.

Predictably, there was mass unemployment amongst the day workers who sewed the dresses for the upper classes, but La Maison Gagelin weathered the storm, surviving on the sale of cheaper materials. The highly skilled sales team of Charles Worth and Marie Vernet kept their jobs, and even began to think tentatively about marrying once the economy picked up.

Their professional partnership had quickly grown into something much more personal. Marie found the handsome young Englishman slightly arrogant, and his easy charm with women customers might have frightened her if he had been French. But he wasn't attempting to sweet-talk the ladies into doing anything except buy. Meanwhile he found Marie exotically French, combining Parisian *savoir-faire* with provincial good sense, and Latin seductiveness with an alluring shyness.

There was a deeper level to their chemistry. They had had very similar childhoods. They had both been forced to start full-time work very young, whereas their elder siblings had been luckier. They felt united in past misfortune, and were both survivors. They also worked superbly together, and shared an unerring ambition to succeed in the trade they knew so well. Instinctively, they recognized that they were soulmates.

ϖϖϖ

The recession was quickly brought to an end by Louis-Napoléon, a man who was determined to prove that the Bonaparte family was better for France than the royals had been.

As president, he gave his personal support – and a massive subsidy of 600,000 francs – to the huge 1849 *Exposition nationale des produits de l'industrie agricole et manufacturière* (National Exhibition of Products of the Agricultural and Manufacturing Industries). This was a trade fair, with almost 5,500 exhibitors displaying their wares in a purpose-built hall on the Champs-Elysées. Throughout the summer of that year, the *Exposition nationale* brought visitors flocking back to Paris to see the best that France and its colonies could offer, in food, chemicals, ceramics, machines – and, of course, fabrics.

Sadly, Marie Aglaé Gagelin was missing out on this revival. She died in February 1848, aged 33. Her mother Marie Élisabeth was almost 60 now, and so their best salesman, Charles Worth, was appointed *premier commis* – principal sales clerk. It was true that he had ten years' experience in the rag trade, but even so, it was a spectacular promotion for a young man of only 22, and a foreigner at that.

The longer-serving Marie Vernet was forced to accept that her male colleague took precedence in the new hierarchy, but she did so with good grace, especially because this sudden salary rise prompted Charles to propose marriage.

ϖϖϖ

Despite Paris's louche reputation, things had probably been fairly chaste between Charles and Marie before the proposal. They did not live together. Marie was still lodging in the rue Saint Marc, around the corner from La Maison Gagelin, where her mother had originally found accommodation when the three Vernets arrived in Paris. There, Marie had no doubt been left under the scrutiny of a dictatorial concierge.

Charles was housed closer to Gagelin, at number 89 rue de Richelieu, above the dressmaker's shop that used to supply Joséphine Bonaparte.

In any case, Marie, a staunch church-goer, knew that a girl with a steady job and decent working conditions (by the standards of the time) would have been foolish to compromise her lifestyle by getting pregnant – especially with a man barely better off than she was.

Once Marie had accepted Charles' proposal of marriage, the two fiancés became the President and First Lady of Gagelin's shop floor. And their new status encouraged them to begin some ground-breaking experiments.

Charles had decided that the dresses Marie wore

needed to be more simply cut if they were to look good beneath a shawl or cloak, or when accessorized with a hat and scarf. They were too fussy, too French, and needed a more dashing – more English – touch.

Motivated by the magnificent fabrics in the shop, and inspired even further by Sunday visits to the artworks at the Louvre, Charles began to sketch dresses with Marie in mind. He didn't dare stray too far from the fashions of the day. He kept his designs simple, making them stand out with a certain sophistication in the outlines and an inventive, though subtler, use of trimmings.

Sitting in a café on Sundays (after Marie had been to Mass), they would refine the drawings, and decide which fabrics would best suit the design – if they could ever afford to get them made.

After a few months, Charles paid out of his own pocket for a few of his dresses to be cut and sewn in the Gagelin workshops – to fit Marie, of course. Initially these were in plain white muslin, almost like blank canvases. They were eye-catchingly designed but still sober in colour, as befitted the dress code of a *demoiselle de magasin*, and Marie began wearing them to work, becoming Paris's most sharply-dressed sales assistant – and in effect the French fashion industry's first-ever full-time model. In the past, a dressmaker would often ask a salesgirl to put on a dress, to show a client how it moved, but Marie was now constantly on display in Charles's designs.

This new role was so innovative that, when Marie later developed and formalized it, no one seems to have known what to call her. Salesgirls had often put on dresses to show clients how the garment looked. When they did this, they were simply called '*sosies*' (doubles or lookalikes), because they were of a very similar size and shape to the individual costumer buying the outfit. Marie, though, was doing something different: she was being herself, displaying a dress so that potential customers could imagine what it *might* look like on them *if* they ordered it. There wasn't a name for this until 1860 when a French journalist referred to her as a *'mannequin'*. It might not have been meant flatteringly – this was, after all, the word for an inanimate dummy. The term derives from the Flemish *'mannekijn'* meaning 'little man'[15], and was first applied to clothing in 16th-century Flanders when small dolls were used to show dress designs in miniature. Marie is generally acknowledged to be the first life-size *'mannequin vivant'*, or living model.

Unlike today's skeleton-like fashion models, Marie was amply proportioned, a look that was very much the trend in mid-century Paris. To be thin meant you were either poor or dying of some wasting disease, or both. And in one of Charles' dresses, even cut from plain fabric, the dark-haired, blue-eyed Marie looked as classy as any of her rich customers. The outfits were so well cut, and they fitted her so perfectly, that they were always strikingly elegant.

ധധധ

Getting the dresses made up was an inspired piece of private initiative. These gowns were not for sale, so it was a case of teasing customers by creating a demand that could not be satisfied. Many of Gagelin's customers noticed the dresses, only to be told that unfortunately the designs were not commercially available … yet.

The fiancés began to badger Octave Opigez, Marie

---

[15] Hence also the name Manneken Pis for Brussels' famous statue of a urinating baby.

Gagelin's widower, to sell Charles's dresses at the shop. The idea was that clients who liked the way Marie wore one of Worth's creations could order the dress for themselves, to be made in Gagelin's fabrics and sold directly by the store.

By this time, one of Paris's best-known dressmakers, Madame Rodger, had already begun supplying the material for the clothes she made. However, she was not bold enough to suggest that she would also design the garments. She did things the old way, copying existing patterns. The innovation that Charles now suggested to Octave Opigez was that La Maison Gagelin would control every step in the dressmaking process from conception to delivery, selling its materials, its labour and of course Charles's talent.

At first Opigez was reticent. In his mind, the only reason why fabric shops printed catalogues of dress designs was to inspire clients to buy the required lengths of material, so that they could then order the actual clothes from a *couturière*. None of La Maison Gagelin's direct competitors were selling dresses or even dress patterns, so how could Opigez afford to create this new side to his business?

On top of all this, Opigez might well have found it strange that a man would want to indulge in what was then strictly a woman's activity. The French word for a dressmaker was *couturière*, feminine, not the masculine *couturier*.

It wasn't until 1851, spurred on by demand from trusted customers, that Opigez tentatively allowed Worth to implement his plan and advertise his dresses for sale. However, it was only a partial victory, because Opigez insisted that the clients should choose their own fabrics. Charles's true ambition was to impose his personal choice of materials and trimmings for each design and each individual customer.

But the initial scheme was so successful that Charles upped his demands, and he was finally given the go-ahead to open a whole new department commercializing his dresses. From now on, La Maison Gagelin would sell Worth's creations made in Worth's choice of colours and fabrics, with the finishings that he personally recommended for each client. And, being based in a fabric shop, Charles had access to a far better selection of materials than any of the traditional dressmakers in Paris. He could even suggest new motifs and colours to the textile manufacturers who visited Gagelin touting for orders. In other words, Charles had succeeded in putting the dressmaker at the epicentre of the textile industry – it was a revolutionary concept.

ʊʊʊ

A sewing workshop was set up in La Maison Gagelin and in-house seamstresses were hired. Space was cleared for a showroom, where a brand-new profession was formally created: Marie now spent all her working days showing off Charles's dresses to customers. There was no raised catwalk yet, but the fashion show had been invented.

Today's catwalk models often parade semi-naked in front of their audience, but Marie was not encouraged to show any unnecessary flesh. When modelling short-sleeved or low-cut outfits, any bare skin was covered up with a black silk body stocking worn beneath the dress. To reveal anything below the neck or above the wrist in a shop would have been considered unseemly. And in mid-19th-century France, ladies' calves and ankles were always invisible to the general public, anyway. This silk cover-up technique must have made modelling a black dress complicated, but for the moment it was as revealing as the profession could get.[16]

Even using this new modelling technique, it wasn't always plain sailing – or selling. There were recalcitrant women who hung on to the traditional way of using dressmakers. They would be escorted into Charles's showroom only to declare that their maid had brought along an old ball gown that was to be copied in a new fabric. Sometimes women would even bring in a dress and ask for a few alterations to the shape or the trimmings to give the tired garment fresh life.

Stick-in-the-mud attitudes like this would get Charles bristling. Combining his natural sense of superiority in matters of taste with the smoothest of sales patter, he would enquire if Madame was *completely* sure about copying or refurbishing her old dress, and summon Marie through the curtains from the fitting room. She would be modelling one of his creations that used Gagelin's fabrics in an eye-catchingly new way – strips of material gathered to enhance the bust or the shoulders, pleats where none had been seen before, bold designs within the fabric itself. He found ways of applying plain silk ribbons that made the simplest dress shapes shout out with originality, and he shocked Parisians with his use of colours – pink with black, purple with yellow, or waves of sheer shimmering silver. Gradually, Charles's art and Marie's display began winning over the sceptics.

---

[16] It is not entirely clear whether Marie began wearing these black body stockings while still working for Gagelin. It is sometimes said that the Worths created this whole culture of modelling only after setting up their own business. But it seems more likely that their plans were all well formulated before they left Gagelin.

Charles also started to change the overall silhouette of Parisian ladies – he increased the size of the cloaks that women commonly wore at the time. Instead of short capes, he designed floor-length cloaks that were coats in all but name, with large hoods and colourful linings. This meant selling more fabric, which naturally appealed to his employer.

Charles's department was such a success that in May 1851, several of his dresses were sent to adorn the company's stand at the Great Exhibition of the Works of Industry of All Nations, held in London's new Crystal Palace. In other words, the 25-year-old Charles Worth's creations were representing one of France's most fashionable fabric merchants at the world's biggest-ever trade fair. It was a gigantic accolade for a man who, only a handful of years earlier, had arrived jobless in Paris.

According to Charles and Marie's son Jean-Philippe, the Worth designs were too daring for the judges, who 'criticised [them] with the utmost harshness and severity.' But he seems to have been trying to exaggerate his father's struggle to make a name for himself. In fact, the official Jury Report singled out Charles's 'dresses of elegant style.' The visitors to the Great Exhibition were also won over, and orders came rushing in.

Feeling decidedly more reassured about the future, on 21 June 1851, the two former apprentices, Charles Worth and Marie Vernet, got married[17] and set up home

---

[17] On the marriage certificate, Charles was listed as a *commis* – a salesman – whereas no profession was given for Marie. This was a common omission: 19th-century French bureaucrats were not particularly interested in a woman's professional achievements. It also must be said that some women preferred to give the impression that they did not *need* to work, rather than admitting to a menial job.

together. According to Worth family records, they initially moved in above the Gagelin shop in the rue de Richelieu. Each partner brought to the marriage about 2,000 francs in savings, the equivalent today of £16,000 in total. It was not a fortune, but now they had stability, and were edging towards independence.

ʊʊʊ

At the same time, France itself was undergoing a profound change. It was in December of that eventful year of 1851 that Louis-Napoléon mounted a *coup d'état* to make himself Emperor. This time, his revolution was relatively peaceful (by French standards): a few barricades were thrown up on the Paris boulevards, about 500 protesters were killed by the army, and a few thousand objectors were transported to the colonies.

But overall, the French people supported the change, which must have revived folk memories of the glory days of the first Bonaparte. The renamed Napoléon III[18] was soon free to proceed with bold plans for modernizing France that included a campaign to boost its industries – notably textiles.

Napoléon III announced his imminent marriage, and amongst the first requirements for this new First Lady of France was a full wardrobe of outfits fit for the Palais des Tuileries, where the Emperor had now taken up residence.

Just a ten-minute stroll away in the rue de Richelieu, a young Anglo-French couple were giving these developments their full attention. For the time being, they were trapped behind the curtain of their famous employer's

---

[18] Napoléon I was Napoléon Bonaparte and Napoléon II was his exiled son who died at the age of 21, never having ruled.

name. La Maison Gagelin received a huge order – but only for fabrics. The Empress's new dresses were to be made by well-known women *couturières*.

All Charles and Marie Worth could do was spend long hours at the shop helping to put together the raw materials for the imperial trousseau. But they were already planning how to emerge centre-stage, and get their talents noticed by France's new Empress, Eugénie.

4 A TRAITOR'S DAUGHTER

The future Empress Eugénie of France, the woman whose patronage would one day make the name Worth famous worldwide, was born María Eugenia Ignacia Agustina de Palafox y Kirkpatrick, in Granada, southern Spain, on 5 May 1826 – seven months after Charles Worth and nine months after Marie Vernet. Her name was aristocratic but it was looked down upon by many Spaniards because the family had betrayed its country by supporting Napoléon Bonaparte's invading French army during the Peninsular War of 1807-14.

The French occupation of Spain had been sadistic, as is graphically illustrated in Francisco Goya's famous painting, *The Third of May 1808*, which depicts surrendering Spaniards being massacred by a French firing squad.

Eugénie's father, Cipriano de Palafox y Portocarrero, count of Teba and Montijo, fought alongside the French against his own countrymen, and later lost his right eye while defending Paris against the British general (a certain Wellington) who had evicted the French from the Iberian Peninsular and chased them back to France.

In short, Eugénie's father was a fully committed traitor, and when Spain regained its independence, the family was exiled from Madrid and forced to live 400 kilometres away in Granada. Cipriano himself was imprisoned from 1823 to 1829, with the right to only one conjugal visit per year. Consequently, Eugénie's paternity was questioned as soon as she was born – a dent in her personal reputation.

ϖϖϖ

Eugénie's mother was also an outsider, half-Scottish and half-Belgian, as was testified by her multilingual maiden name, María Manuela Enriqueta Kirkpatrick de Closeburn y de Grevignée[19].

According to one 19th century French writer, Louise Lacroix, who published a short but antagonistic biography of Eugénie in 1870, María Manuela had 'consoled herself in the arms of numerous lovers who helped her to forget the ugliness and stupidity of her idiotic husband.' Lacroix alleged (probably inaccurately) that Eugénie's biological father was one of these lovers, George Villiers, Earl of Clarendon, the British ambassador to Spain, who 'visited' María Manuela while her husband was locked up in prison.

In 1834, during a civil war in Spain over the succession to the throne, María Manuela took Eugénie and her elder sister, María Francisca, to Paris.

There, between 1835 and 1839, the mother invested a large proportion of her meagre finances sending her girls to a renowned convent school housed in a mansion in

---

[19] Regarding these long noble titles: at that time, European aristocrats used to pile up family names, presumably as a way of remembering which dynasties they no longer needed to marry into.

central Paris, the Hôtel Biron (which is now the Rodin Museum).

The school offered a varied curriculum, including artistic and cultural subjects, priding itself on matching the academic standards of Jesuit boys' schools – an example of post-Revolution French egalitarianism.

At the Hôtel Biron, Eugénie was taught by two exceptional tutors: the author, linguist and historian Prosper Mérimée, who would later write *Carmen*, and one of France's greatest 19th-century novelists, Stendhal.

Stendhal was the author of the famous *Le Rouge et le Noir*, the story of a fervent young admirer of Napoléon Bonaparte who becomes the tutor to some bourgeois children ... and has an affair with the lady of the house.[20]

Eugénie remembered later that Stendhal 'sat us [Eugénie and her elder sister], one on each knee, and told us the stories of Napoléon's campaigns.' These history lessons would have been the perfect preparation for Eugénie's meeting a few years later with her future husband, the great Napoléon's nephew, Napoléon III.

In 1836, released from prison, Eugénie's father paid a brief visit to his family in Paris, and was apparently worried to see Eugénie's serious, nun-like demeanour. He decided to take radical action and sent her to a military-style academy where she learned horse-riding, fencing and – unusually for a girl at the time – swimming. The future Empress's education was completed during a short stay at a school near Bristol, where she learnt fluent English.

---

[20] It is not clear whether Stendhal extended his literary ideas into his relations with Eugénie's mother.

In 1839, Eugénie's father died, leaving the family in some financial embarrassment. Her mother therefore became determined to snare suitable husbands for her two French-educated teenage daughters. She dragged them around Europe, including Belgium and England, in search of eligible bachelors.

Both girls ripened into alluring womanhood, with attractive figures, red-tinted blond hair, and fine ivory features.

Here is a description of Eugénie at the age of 16, from the memoirs of a French writer called Maxime Du Camp. He recounts how he was at a house party just outside Paris in 1842, enjoying a cigar with the distinguished male guests, when a girl burst into the billiard room …

> She jumped up on to the table and began a flamenco dance. Swinging her hips, thrusting out her chest, clicking her fingers, her head inclined, her eyes half-closed, she laughed as she kicked away the billiard balls. Lord Howden grabbed her calf, but she slapped him on the head, leapt towards the door and disappeared. It was Eugénie-Marie de Guzman de Montijo, countess of Téba.[21] Her white skin, her blond hair with its reddish highlights, her blue eyes and mournful expression, her fresh lips, the burgeoning curves already visible beneath her bodice, her supple waist and her long fingers, all combined to make her a most

---

[21] Du Camp gives Eugénie the titles she would have in later life. While her mother was alive, she was not yet a countess. As a younger woman, she was known in France simply as Eugénie de Montijo.

attractive creature. It was impossible not to admire her, even though it was obvious that she craved admiration.

At the age of 17, the vivacious Eugénie almost married brilliantly. She fell in love with her cousin, the fabulously wealthy Jaime, duke of Alba. The two exchanged passionate letters – she wrote 'There is nothing I would not do for you, so please put me to the test. I would even dishonour myself to prove the strength of my love' – and it became public knowledge that they were lovers.

However, Eugénie's mother had other plans, and informed the young duke that he would be marrying her elder daughter, Eugénie's sister, María Francisca. The duke hesitated for a while, but then announced his decision – he would follow the countess's instructions. The heartbroken Eugénie ran away to a convent and tried to become a nun, until the mother superior managed to convince her that a failed romance was not the same as a religious vocation.

To get over her humiliation, Eugénie took to frequenting matadors, attending their training sessions in the bullring and provoking (almost certainly fake) rumours about an affair with a famous toreador called El Chicanero. Fearing for her daughter's reputation, Eugénie's mother whisked the tempestuous teenager away, to Bordeaux, Hamburg and England.

ϖϖϖ

Then in 1848, after years of wandering Europe vainly looking for a suitable match, France suddenly became the place-to-be for an attractive, unmarried female fan of the Bonapartes.

The country had just undergone its fifth or sixth revolution (depending on how you count) since 1789. Louis-Napoléon Bonaparte was now president, meaning that suddenly, Eugénie and her mother had a very well-placed French ally. The Bonapartes had never forgotten the one-eyed Cipriano's service to the Napoleonic cause, so it was entirely natural for his widow and daughter to come to France and join the family celebrations.

ധധധ

Arriving early in 1849, Eugénie's mother quickly got herself invited into the entourage of Mathilde, the notorious niece of the former emperor Napoléon Bonaparte. Mathilde was renowned for her riotous *salons* and stormy amorous life. She was married but living openly with a lover. Even so, she had the official title of *maîtresse de maison* (lady of the house) at the presidential palace, the Élysée, the new home of her cousin Louis-Napoléon.

It was common knowledge that he had a long-term live-in lover, an Englishwoman called Harriet Howard, who had financed his recent political campaign. But everyone also knew that he had no intention of marrying Harriet. She was a commoner, a widowed former actress – not marriage material for a French president.

So Louis-Napoléon was probably the best catch in Paris, and Eugénie, fully aware of her charms, seems to have decided that he was catchable.

Inevitably, Mathilde ended up introducing Eugénie to Louis-Napoléon, and from their very first meeting, she began to play hard to get. The president offered Eugénie his arm for a stroll around the garden, but she declined, telling him that, *politesse oblige*, he should accompany her mother instead. The stratagem worked – next day, he sent the young lady a bouquet of flowers.

This in itself was neither exceptional nor flattering. Louis-Napoléon was a shameless *coureur de jupons*, a 'petticoat-chaser', so it was not unusual for him to pursue a woman, especially one as young, exotic and beautiful as Eugénie. But she was determined to make herself exceptional – by continuing to turn him down.

On New Year's Eve, 1849, as midnight struck, Louis-Napoléon announced, 'Everyone must kiss,' and made a bee[22] line for Eugénie. 'It's the custom in France,' he informed her.

'Not in Spain,' she replied, curtsying out of range.

ʊʊʊ

Over the next couple of years, Eugénie and her mother would travel back and forth between Paris and the chic watering holes of Europe, and each time they returned to France, Louis-Napoléon would be waiting with flowers and compliments. He courted other women all the time, but he never forgot Eugénie.

Such persistence definitely *was* flattering, because during that period, Louis-Napoléon was also busy restructuring France's entire political system. This was the time when President Bonaparte became Napoléon III and the Second Republic became the Second Empire. And yet, against the background of this political upheaval, the self-crowned Emperor still found time to mount his siege on an apparently impregnable Spanish citadel. Frustratingly for him, Eugénie continued to hold out. Perhaps she had heard the quip by her suitor's elderly uncle Jérôme, one of Napoléon Bonaparte's

---

[22] A pun for historians: the bee was one of the emblems of the Bonaparte family. The other was the eagle.

brothers: 'My nephew will marry the first woman who captivates him but refuses her favours.'

Eugénie began to reel him in. Soon after Napoléon III's elevation to imperial status, she received an invitation to one of his hunting weekends in the forest of Compiègne. And at these hunts, all the women guests were fair game. Or so the Emperor assumed.

According to the sharp-tongued biographer Louise Lacroix, Eugénie's entrance was carefully staged:

> Mounted upon a beautiful Andalusian, she made her appearance amongst the hunters, her graceful, slender waist tightly enclosed in an elegant riding jacket [...] Her legs and thighs were outlined in skin-tight grey trousers,[23] which sculpted and enhanced their delicious curves, hinting at other, even more voluptuous love treasures, and she aroused the most vigorous enthusiasm in the connoisseurs whose eyes devoured her. From that instant, the libidinous gaze of Louis Bonaparte [i.e. Napoléon III], until then secretive and distracted, focused on her and did not budge. She saw the effect she had provoked, and swore to profit from it, accentuating her coquettish moves in order to seduce the heart of her imperial host, whom she was determined to conquer, exactly as her ambitious and resourceful mother had recommended [...]
>
> Several times, the intrepid Amazon, her

---

[23] Having been to the military-style academy, Eugénie had learned some boyish habits, including wearing riding breeches instead of a dress, which most women wore on horseback.

pink lips half-open to reveal her pearly-white teeth, her nostrils dilated, her eyes flashing, her golden hair gleaming in the sun on her white shoulders, shot through the imperial group like an arrow, and then disappeared. And every time the amorous monarch tried to follow her, she rode away.

When, at the end of the day, Napoléon III moved in for the kill, he was fobbed off yet again. The Emperor asked Eugénie: 'How does one get to your bedroom?' to which she famously replied: 'Through the chapel.'

Napoléon III did not give up hope of a brief encounter, and even resorted to having a secret door built into the wall of the bedroom where Eugénie slept at the château. According to Maxime Du Camp, the next time Eugénie was a guest there:

> In the middle of the night, Mademoiselle de Montijo saw the Emperor entering her room. She kept her calm. She invited him to sit down, and lectured him: "I thought I was in the house of a gentleman." He begged, he pleaded, he wept, he lost his temper – all to no avail. He left the room by the same secret route, taking with him his brief humiliation and a love that robbed him of all free will.

Eventually, the new Emperor became resigned to the fact that he would have to marry the Spanish seductress if he wanted to sleep with her. And after all, she was not a bad bridal candidate: Spanish nobility with Bonapartist leanings, at a time when Spain itself was unstable and potentially ripe for regime change. A Franco-Spanish Bonaparte heir might end up as King of Spain, as

Napoléon III's uncle Joseph had been.

Predictably, there was fierce opposition amongst the French to the idea of the Emperor's marriage to a Spanish countess, particularly from those who thought that a match between a Bonaparte and a member of the ancient French royal family (that is, a relative of the guillotined King Louis XVI) would be a better way of uniting the country by combining France's two most powerful political dynasties.

Others assumed that a French Emperor should marry into a *foreign* royal family, as Napoléon I had done in 1810, when he granted himself a speedy divorce from Joséphine and married Princess Maria Ludovica of Austria.

On a much more personal level, the Emperor's cousin Mathilde was against his marriage because it would rob her of her rank as *maîtresse de maison*. Mathilde was also jealous – she had refused to marry Louis-Napoléon back in the days when it looked much less likely that he would ever come to power in France.

ʊʊʊ

As soon as the Emperor's crush on the foreign countess became public knowledge, so did the injurious gossip about her, and rumours of her past love affairs with assorted nobles and matadors were broadcast all over Paris.

The hostility seems to have crystallized on the evening of 12 January 1853, when, during a ball at the Palais des Tuileries, Eugénie was publicly insulted by a certain Julie Fortoul, the wife of the Minister of Education, who called the Spanish countess an '*aventurière*', a gold-digger.

Later that evening, Eugénie confided in the Emperor: 'I have been insulted as never before, without anyone to defend me. Tomorrow my mother and I will leave Paris, and you will hear of us no more.'

It was a master stroke. Napoléon III went to see Eugénie's mother the very next day, and formally requested her daughter's hand in marriage. He wrote to his cousin Mathilde that, 'appreciating [Eugénie's] solid and good qualities, I have taken the irrevocable decision to marry her. Once she is Empress [...] her position and conduct will command respect.'

In reply, Mathilde warned him that 'France will find it unflattering that you have not chosen a French wife,' but promised her support anyway.

Events began to move very fast. On 22 January, the Emperor summoned the entire French body politic to the Tuileries, to hear a speech in defence of his choice of bride:

> She whom I have chosen is of noble birth. She is French by her affections, by her education, and by the memory of the blood her father shed for the cause of the Empire [Napoléon I's regime]. [...] Catholic and pious, she will say exactly the same prayers as I do for France's happiness; gracious and good-hearted, she will, I hope, bring back to life the virtues of the Empress Joséphine [Napoléon I's first wife, who also had no royal connections].
>
> So let me declare to the whole of France: I have chosen a woman whom I love and respect, instead of a stranger, an alliance with whom would have brought both advantages and sacrifices.

It sounds lukewarm, as though he is saying, 'This foreigner is sexy as well as reasonably suitable, so *pourquoi pas?*' Not an auspicious start.

The civil wedding took place on 29 January, followed by a religious ceremony the next day in Notre-Dame cathedral.

And so an almost exact contemporary of Charles and Marie Worth was installed in the imperial palace. The Worths knew that like them, Eugénie was an outsider in Paris, and would have to fight to win acceptance amongst the French, as Charles had had to do.

The new Empress was also saddled with heavy expectations: the immediate responsibility of becoming a female role model, France's most glamorous, best-dressed woman. Surely she would need help with that?

All eyes were on Eugénie, especially those in the rue de Richelieu.

5 A PERFECT PARISIAN MATCH

As Eugénie settled into the Tuileries, Charles and Marie Worth were consolidating their status as the jewels in the crown of La Maison Gagelin's success. In 1853, its business was beginning to boom under Napoléon III's economic regeneration programme.

The Emperor had turned Paris into a party town. High society was a whirl of garden parties and balls. The new class of bourgeois Parisians were feeling optimistic enough to splash out on clothes for dinner parties, evenings at the theatre and days at the races. Foreign visitors, not wanting to look out of place amongst the Parisians, would order complete wardrobes to wear during their stay.

In the rue de Richelieu, Charles Worth worked non-stop designing dresses, seeking out new fabric patterns, organizing the shop's seamstresses and attending fittings with an unremitting flow of new customers.

According to a British weekly magazine, *The Queen, the Ladies' Newspaper and Court Chronicle*, which told the Worths' story a few years later, Charles realized at this point in his career that:

Miss Flora McFlimsey[24] of Maddison-square and all her friends, who found in Broadway nothing good enough to wear, were coming over to Europe to learn how to dress, and going to Paris for the latest fashions. Mr Worth saw all this and knew where his fortune lay.

In practical terms, Charles felt that all his instincts about how to grow Gagelin's business were being confirmed before his eyes, so that he deserved more recognition, more freedom – and greater rewards.

In July 1853 he convinced his employers to restructure their entire company. The old Maison Gagelin would cease to exist, and be replaced by a new firm with three directors: Octave-François Opigez-Gagelin, Ernest Walles (a Gagelin employee) and the slightly gallicized 'Charles-Frédéric Worth' (also listed in the contract as an employee). The official announcement in the *Gazette des Tribunaux* (court records) informed the public that the trio would 'continue to run the company selling cashmeres, silks, garments and new fashions [...] established in Paris, formerly known as Gagelin.'

This sounds like a sea change in the Worths' fortunes, but there was a revealing clause in the agreement: 'Management will be shared, but Monsieur Opigez is the sole signatory.' There was still, in effect, one boss. Charles would take a fairer proportion of the profits but have no real control over the direction the business was to take.

---

[24] This is a misquote from an 1857 poem, 'Nothing to Wear', by American satirical poet William Allen Butler, making fun of New York's high society ladies. The actual lines read: 'This same Miss McFlimsey, of Madison Square/ The last time we met, was in utter despair/ Because she had nothing whatever to wear.'

Inevitably, as a woman, Marie had no financial share or any control at all.

ഗഗഗ

Charles continued to attract attention for the company. In 1855, Paris held an *Exposition Universelle*, and Gagelin displayed several of his creations. One of these was a *manteau de cour* (court train), a garment for gala occasions. At every imperial ball, women had to wear a train three or four metres in length, as if they were all attending a coronation. Usually these were attached at the waist, but Worth designed a new version, a long train of gold-embroidered silk that hung from the shoulders of the wearer, recalling similar garments worn at the court of the first Napoléon – it was a flattering nod towards the new regime. The *manteau de cour* won a medal at the *Exposition*. But it was awarded to Gagelin, and Charles was apparently indignant that he received no personal recognition.

By this time, his creations were also featuring in fashion magazines. A coloured etching from 1855 in *Le Moniteur des Dames et des Demoiselles* – a journal founded in 1854 that advertised itself as the 'complete guide to ladies' work' – showed two young ladies in enormous crinolines. One of these is a low-cut ball gown, white with flowered borders and a tight blue bodice, the other a high-necked dress in lush purple and black. Both were credited as 'Toilettes[25] de la Maison Gagelin'. Charles

---

[25] This does not refer to lavatories, of course. *Toilette* is the general term for a full outfit of clothes. It will crop up frequently in this book.

was not yet being named, but he was making his mark. [26]

Meanwhile, Marie would come to work every day in one of Charles's dresses, even when she thought that the design did not suit her or was too unconventional. Despite her growing experience as a model, she still felt uncomfortable being the constant centre of attention, but she diligently stuck to her task, working even longer hours now that she, via her husband Charles, had a bigger stake in the company.

Modelling 19th-century dresses was no easy task. The bodices and waistbands were horrifically tight. Marie was no stick insect under normal circumstances, and in 1853, she had to truss herself up during her first pregnancy, with their son Gaston. In 1856, she had to repeat the ordeal for the second son, Jean-Philippe.

What was worse, the Worths were living out, in la rue Neuve-Saint-Augustin (now the rue Saint-Augustin). Their apartment was only a few minutes' walk away from the shop, but it was too far to nip home to eat at lunchtime. The Worths would often skip lunch or eat quickly on the premises, with no chance to relax. And Marie needed somewhere to loosen her stays and take a real break at mid-day.

In addition, she had to spend a long time every morning getting ready to go on public view, so her working day started a good hour before she even got into the shop at 8AM. And the opening hours were punishingly long – Gagelin usually closed at 8PM. After more than twelve hours imprisoned in her corset, Marie would be feeling ill, even when she wasn't pregnant.

---

[26] It was perhaps natural that the magazine should notice Charles's designs because its offices were at number 92 rue de Richelieu, down the road from Maison Gagelin. (This was also the building that housed the Boulangerie Viennoise where French croissants had first been sold.)

It is a measure of her patience and work ethic that she put up with this hardship until sometime in 1858, when she took the initiative of going to Octave Opigez and asking to rent an apartment on the company premises. There were plenty of trainees' rooms upstairs above the shop – some of those could easily be turned into a family home, she argued. She and her husband were more loyal than ever to La Maison Gagelin and surely deserved to have their daily lives made more comfortable?

It is easy to imagine the down-to-earth *Auvergnate*, resplendent in one of her husband's latest creations but exhausted by her workload, stating her case.

But for once, her sales pitch fell on deaf ears. Opigez refused, triggering a monumental decision: Charles and Marie tendered their resignation which, inexplicably, was accepted. Octave Opigez was clearly too hands-off to realize how much of Gagelin's reputation with customers depended on personal contact with the Worths, and on Charles's growing skill as a designer. In his memoir, Jean-Philippe Worth goes further, saying that Opigez was 'stiff-necked to the point of stupidity.'

ღღღ

The catalyst for the couple's ultimatum was a Swede, the son of a rich banker. This was Otto Gustaf Bobergh, born in 1821 in Stockholm, an itinerant artist and fabric designer. As a young man he had worked for a Swedish silk merchant, then spent time in Paris and London, before returning to Paris for the *Exposition Universelle* of 1855, where he represented the Compagnie Lyonnaise, one of Gagelin's chief competitors in the drapery trade. He was, like Charles and Marie, a salesman with ambitions far beyond his station – the difference being that he had access to the funds to realize them.

Otto, Charles and Marie decided to branch out on their own. Otto borrowed money from his rich relatives, and in 1858 the two men signed a ten-year contract (only males signed business contracts in mid-19th-century France) to create a new fashion house, Worth et Bobergh.[27]

They hired 20 seamstresses – including at least one who was tempted away from a stable job with Gagelin – and rented an apartment on the first floor of a building in the rue de la Paix ('peace street'), which was originally called rue Napoléon but had been re-baptized in 1814 to celebrate the peace treaty signed that year between France, Britain and the other European powers.

The rue da la Paix was a thoroughfare with an international reputation. Rich tourists from all over the world were attracted to the Hôtel Mirabeau at number 8, Hôtel Westminster Paris at number 13 and the Hôtel des Îles Britanniques at 22. Foreign dignitaries rode along the street on their way to visit the imperial couple at the Palais des Tuileries.

Now an Anglo-Franco-Swedish business took up residence at number 7.

The building had two shopfronts, one on either side of the main entrance. The Worths would later take over the right-hand shop, but for the moment Charles and Bobergh signed a lease for an upstairs space that combined fitting room, workshop and accommodation

---

[27] The company kept its brand name until 1870, but clients commonly referred to their dresses as being made 'by Worth'. Otto Bobergh seems to have been rapidly eclipsed as a designer and to have welcomed the role of business manager and silent partner, living comfortably while watching his investment skyrocket in value.

for the Worths and their two young children. This set-up allowed Charles and Marie to continue their habit of working all hours.

ඏඏඏ

It was an opportune time to be launching a business because Napoleon III's Second Empire was at its most effervescent. Members of the affluent establishment wanted to be seen looking chic every day and all evening on the wide pavements of Paris's boulevards, at the opera, at parties or in packed ballrooms. Fortunes were being spent on fashion.

The industrial revolution had kick-started in France and new fabrics were being invented, like bengaline, a rayon-cotton mix that looked like silk. Weaving machines had also made old fabrics cheaper. This was the case for taffeta[28], an ancient cloth made of woven silk, or silk and rayon, that was highly fashionable in the mid-19th century.

Damask – silk with a pattern of the same colour woven into it – became much more varied and ambitious in its motifs with the freedom that machine weaving offered. Charles Worth started to experiment with dresses made of outrageous damasks: a woman could sport a life-size heron on the front of her skirt, or her bodice could become a field of ripening wheat. In an album preserved in the Victoria & Albert museums there is a watercolour, probably painted by one of the artists Charles used to make a record of his creations, of a woman wearing a dress with a spookily surreal flower

---

[28] Taffeta had long been appreciated for its strength combined with lightness. Joseph Montgolfier used it to make his first hot-air balloons.

design. Toxic-looking pink-and-white lilies, as big as the woman's hand, hang from two eerie black branches that climb from floor to hip. The effect must have been original, dazzling and impossible to ignore.

There were brand-new colours, too. France had just fought a brief war with Austria and in June 1859 had won two battles, Solferino and Magenta[29]. These victories inspired not only a surge in patriotism but also two fashionable new hues that everyone wanted to wear – a bright Solferino blue and a purplish Magenta red.

ʊʊʊ

Worth et Bobergh was launched in a spirit of huge optimism. Opportunities were there to be seized.

The shop began selling fine fabrics – silk, cashmere, lace, fur – as well as marketing Charles Worth's dress designs. However, business was slow at first. The rue de la Paix was chic but it was not at the heart of the fabric-selling neighbourhood. The perfumier Pierre Guerlain, who created fragrances for the imperial couple, including the romantic-sounding Bouquet Napoléon, had recently moved his headquarters to number 15. There were a few renowned jewellers nearby[30] – but no other drapers to tempt fabric buyers into the area.

In February 1859, there was an article on the back page of the Parisian daily newspaper *Vert-Vert*. It reads like advertorial:

In July, when Messrs Worth and Bobergh

---

[29] Predictably both of these victories also gave rise to Parisian street names. Boulevard Magenta was baptized in 1859 and rue de Solferino in 1866.
[30] Not yet Cartier, which arrived at number 13 in 1899.

opened their *maison*, a large proportion of their circulars did not reach their destination, as almost all the people comprising their clientele were absent from Paris at that time.

Every day, questions are asked, and ladies complain that they were not informed about the opening of this new store.

Messrs Worth and Bobergh have asked us to announce that their establishment specializing in Dresses, Coats and Furs is situated at 7 rue de la Paix, on the first floor, on the former site of the Timbre[31].

If the article was a tongue-in-cheek attempt to explain their slow start, it feels awkward. It was true that not all Charles's clients had followed him from Gagelin – a major disappointment. Worse, some of those who did migrate with him expected discounts now that he had cut out the middleman.

The new shop urgently needed to attract fresh customers if it wanted to take advantage of the favourable economic climate. In this, Marie Worth played a vital role. As well as modelling new designs in the showroom, she began acting as a roving sales operator.

Whenever Charles and Marie went out walking, she would be wearing a Worth creation, just in case a passer-by stopped them and inquired about her unique outfit. The summer of 1859 was hot, and it was uncomfortable to be strolling through steamy Paris in an all-enveloping dress, but stalwart Marie did her duty.

Even so, despite Marie's open-air catwalk shows, sales did not pick up. The scorching weather chased even

---

[31] 'The Stamp.' This was the name of Paris's Centre of Public Finances, which had recently moved near the Palais Royal.

more Parisians than usual out of the city. As autumn approached, Charles and Marie were scraping a living on the customers they had poached from Gagelin.

At last, though, the wealthy began to return to Paris from their country retreats. On fine days, the boulevards and parks were alive with promenading couples, and suddenly the winter ball season was occupying all fashion-conscious minds. Everyone who was anyone began to dream of an invitation to the weekly highpoint of the social calendar – a *soirée* at the Tuileries Palace. Charles and Marie Worth realized that this was where the survival of their new business lay. All the rich ladies in Paris needed a fabulous dress that would catch the eye of the Empress, and Charles had to be the man who designed that outfit.

There was also an even more glittering prize to be won. Every dressmaker in Paris wanted Eugénie herself as a client. Charles had been bitterly disappointed when he saw the old-fashioned dresses made out of the fabrics that Gagelin had sold for the Empress's wedding trousseau. Created by the court *couturières* Mesdames Palmyre and Vignon, they were (in Charles's opinion) much too elaborate to be truly elegant. Eugénie was undoubtedly glamorous, and had succeeded in establishing herself as France's First Lady of fashion, but there was a lot of room for improvement.

The three outsiders in Paris had not yet met in person, but at the end of 1859, their orbits were perfectly aligned: Charles and Marie needed Eugénie, and she (though she didn't yet know it) needed them.

ღღღ

Eugénie was by now at the pinnacle of French society, but she was feeling vulnerable. Her adaptation to life at the heart of Napoléon III's court had not been an easy one.

She had foreseen the problems ahead as soon as she signed the marriage certificate.

After her civil wedding she wrote to her sister: 'Soon I will be alone here, without any friends [...] I, who was mad about freedom, am chaining up my life. Never alone, never free, and subject to court etiquette of which I will be the main victim.'

One of Eugénie's key tasks as Empress was, of course, to provide an heir. She suffered a miscarriage, but then on 16 March 1856, she gave birth to a son. True to form, her most vicious critic Louise Lacroix wrote that Eugénie had borne a child 'thanks to the collaboration of the numerous good-looking officers in her entourage.'

In truth, it was difficult, impossible even, for an imperial wife to be unfaithful – informers were everywhere, and the French attitude to an adulterous woman was not as tolerant as it was towards wandering males[32].

The rumour-mongers accused Eugénie of having affairs with servants, soldiers and practically any male with access to the Tuileries. France's most revered writer of the time, Victor Hugo, wrote that 'the Eagle' (referring to the Bonaparte family emblem) 'had married a *cocotte*' (the term for a high-class prostitute). And a satirical song had been doing the rounds of Paris ever since the wedding, alleging that: 'If he [Napoléon III] finds her virginity, she must have had two.'

In fact, it was the Emperor who had started straying.

---

[32] According to Napoleonic law, a wife would only sue for divorce if her husband actually installed his mistress in the marital home.

He confessed to his cousin Mathilde: 'I worked at being a good husband for six months,' before returning to his serial philandering. He took up with a glamorous official mistress, a teenaged Italian noblewoman called Virginia, countess of Castiglione.

Wagging tongues all over Paris were alleging that, in any case, sexual contact between Eugénie and her husband was over. Eugénie's labour had been painful and very long – 48 hours – doctors had feared for both mother and baby. And it seems that this traumatic experience, combined with Napoléon's adultery, killed the imperial sex life.

If this was a blow to Eugénie's self-esteem, she compensated by focussing on her public image, more particularly by filling her wardrobe. After all, it was part of her job. She was an Empress and had to dress like one. But even this attracted criticism. She was targeted by her detractors for being a frivolous Marie-Antoinette imitator and given the nickname of '*la fée chiffon*', the fabric fairy.

It seems slightly ludicrous to criticize a woman for making herself look noticeable when her very role was to stand out in a crowd. Queen Elizabeth II of England used to say that she chose the startling colours of the outfits she wore on public occasions so that she would be the most visible person at any occasion: 'If I wore beige, no one would notice me.'[33]

One of Eugénie's ladies-in-waiting, Amélie Carette, made this point in her memoirs, *Souvenirs intimes de la cour des Tuileries* (*Intimate memories of the Tuileries Court*):

---

[33] For more details of Queen Elizabeth's wardrobe, and more of her self-mocking quips, see my book *Elizabeth II, Queen of Laughs*.

The Empress's taste for dresses and luxuries as often been discussed, with passionate exaggeration. Luxury is an obligatory tool for sovereigns [...] The elegance of her clothing is the first criterion in the judgement of a woman; and if some people reproach the sovereign for the variety and luxuriousness of her clothing, most would complain about her appearance if it failed to match up to the tastes and demands of our times.

Carette went even further and suggested that this imperial dressing-up had a beneficial trickle-down effect in French society: 'From the luxury of the rich is born the comfort of the poor.'

Here, she is doubtless going a bit too far, but Napoléon III seems to have agreed to a certain extent. He was keen to present a glamorous modern image for his new empire, in contrast to his deposed predecessor, King Louis-Philippe, who had toned everything down and tried to look like a man of the people – a 'beige' kind of monarch. Eugénie embodied glamour, so she was only fulfilling her husband's wishes.

Nevertheless, according to another of Eugénie's critics, Maxime du Camp, the Emperor complained openly about her sartorial excesses, and even commissioned a satirical operetta in which the heroine wore a comically huge crinoline, the Empress's trademark outfit.

Du Camp alleged that, worse than making herself look comical, Eugénie was causing depravity amongst French womanhood: 'Possessing admirable shoulders and a splendid bosom, she wore outrageous *décolletés*[34], and all the other women imitated her.' He felt forced to add a complaint that 'even the ugliest old hags showed off what they didn't have.'

We can see these 'outrageous *décolletés*' in a sumptuous group portrait, *Empress Eugénie Surrounded by Her Ladies-in-Waiting*, painted in 1855 by the German artist Franz Xaver Winterhalter, the most sought-after — and flattering — society portraitist of the time[35]. The picture shows a magnificently attired, regally poised Eugénie sitting in the centre of a bouquet of impeccably coiffed, porcelain-skinned noblewomen, all of them bare-shouldered above their vast crinolines. It was a scene that harked back ostensibly to the elitist days of Marie-Antoinette, and it probably had French republicans calling for the guillotine to be brought out of storage. But however frivolous and expensive it was, the painting was part of France's display at that year's Paris *Exposition Universelle*. Eugénie was being used as a symbol of the nation.

She did her share of waving from carriages and balconies, posing for official family photographs (a booming new fashion), and welcoming guests at palace meet-and-greets. At these, she became famous for her statuesque serenity — which could, of course, have been a symptom of boredom.

But her life was all not all about dressing up and showing off. She opened hospitals, and she sometimes ventured incognito, in an unmarked carriage, into the poorer *quartiers* of Paris, and then came home to badger

---

[34] Low-cut neckline. Very fashionable in the mid 19th century, this is one French word that will appear a lot in this book.
[35] In 1843 Winterhalter painted a head-and-shoulders portrait of Queen Victoria that actually succeeded in making her look wantonly sexy.

her husband about the need to improve the living conditions of the working classes.

She was often given weightier tasks. She had to stand in for Napoléon at functions when he was suffering from one of his frequent attacks of gout or rheumatism.

Eugénie also made her mark on the diplomatic scene. At palace *soirées*, she would dance with ambassadors while peppering them with questions about international events. This information could then be shared with her husband and his politicians.

ϖϖϖ

However, between conversations with ambassadors and the occasional taste of power, daily life was not fun for Eugénie. There was little or no privacy in the Palace's inter-connected rooms and corridors, which were constantly full of officials, courtiers, servants and hangers-on. At quiet moments, she must have felt that her life would ultimately be a long descent into middle age and *ennui*, with a strong chance that, like the first Emperor Napoléon, her husband would exchange her for a younger model. She knew very well that the Empress Joséphine had been evicted from the Tuileries Palace at the age of 46 and sent into gardening retirement at Malmaison, a small château outside Paris.

There was also a real danger that Eugénie might end up like Marie-Antoinette. Throughout the 1850s there were assassination attempts on Napoléon III[36]. If there was another revolution, Eugénie was at risk of losing her wardrobe, her status, and possibly her head.

All of which explains why, by 1860, the 34-year-old Eugénie was primed and ready for change. Her

---

[36] For more details, see Chapter 14.

crinolines had got as wide as they could get. She needed a new direction. She was psychologically prepared to rebrand herself as the most exciting, most fashionable, most independent woman in Europe.

Enter, exactly on cue, Charles and Marie Worth.

6 AN AUSTRIAN AID PACKAGE

It is a measure of how great the Worth reputation later became that there is strong competition to claim the credit for introducing Charles's creations to the Empress. And sadly for Valérie Feuillet – the client whom we saw in the Prologue, waking Charles and Marie at dawn to demand a ball dress – she is usually gazumped by more famous society ladies.

In an article in 1889, the French newspaper *Le Figaro* told it like this: 'Presented to the Empress by Madame de Pourtalès, he [Charles Worth] soon became not only the provider, but the inspirer of her outfits.'

Charles Worth himself remembered things the same way. In the Rochester *Union and Advertiser* of 11 March 1895 he was quoted as saying that Gagelin 'was extensively patronized by the ladies of the Faubourg St Germain, and one of them introduced me to the Countess de Pourtalès, through whose influence I first submitted one of my creations to the Empress.'

Mélanie de Pourtalès was a young high-society beauty (she was 24 in 1860), a familiar at the court of Eugénie and Napoléon III. She was the daughter of a French financier, and had married into a Swiss banking family. As such, she was exactly the type of person who rose to the top of Second Empire society. She was also relatively daring for her time – there is a photo of her in 1863 carrying a shotgun and wearing a hunting skirt that barely covers her knees, showing off a fine pair of tartan-stockings. It is entirely credible that she could have ordered a dress from the exciting new English designer Charles Worth and shown it to Eugénie.

ϖϖϖ

However, there is an even more likely story told by Jean-Philippe Worth – who of course got most of his information from his father, Charles. Jean-Philippe has the introduction coming from one of Mélanie de Pourtalès's closest friends, the aristocrat Pauline von Metternich, wife of the Austrian ambassador to Paris.

What seems to have happened is that Eugénie had seen several women – including Mesdames Feuillet and de Pourtalès – sporting a Worth dress at an official function, but it was only when the truly noble Pauline von Metternich wore a gown by the same designer that the Empress's curiosity was really piqued.

According to Jean-Philippe Worth, it was Charles and Marie who first spotted Pauline's potential rather than the other way round. One snowy day in December 1859, the Worths were walking near the Tuileries when they saw a convoy of carriages arriving at the Palace. One of them was emblazoned with the twin black eagles of Austria. Inside was a small, dark-haired young woman who, despite the bitter cold, was not wearing a cloak (etiquette prohibited hiding the display of her country's jewels around her neck and wrists). She had driven from the Austrian Embassy just across the Seine, and seemed to be putting on a brave face, smiling to the crowd while freezing to death. This, the Worths learned, was Pauline von Metternich, whose husband (and, incidentally, uncle[37]) Richard had recently been appointed Vienna's representative in France.

But Pauline was much more than the wife of a diplomat. Her full name was Pauline Clementine Marie Walburga, Princess von Metternich-Winneburg zu Bellstein (in Austria, as in other European countries, you were as noble as your name was long). She was the daughter of a Hungarian count and an Austrian princess, and her grandfather (and father-in-law) was the State Chancellor of Austria, Klemens von Metternich.

Something about the 23-year-old Pauline – her obvious vivaciousness, her warm smile – impressed the Worths, and Marie suggested that this new figure on the Parisian social scene might make a potential client for Charles's designs. The Austrian would be keen to make an impact, and would be looking for a local dressmaker.

They quickly got illustrations of Charles's most eye-catching dresses – probably drawn by Otto Bobergh, the more artistic of the partners – bound into a catalogue, and one morning shortly after this first sighting of Pauline, Marie set out for the Austrian Embassy.

It was a bold move. The Embassy was located in an 18th-century palace, the Hôtel de Rothelin Charelais, a former home of the French royal family. The courtyard was entered by a tall archway that usually admitted diplomats' carriages. Almost miraculously, Marie made it past the guards and into the entrance hall, where she managed to speak to one of Princess Pauline's ladies-in-waiting. Marie must have deployed all the seductive sales patter she had learnt *chez* Gagelin, because she convinced

---

[37] Even by 19th-century aristocratic standards, a wedding between niece and uncle bordered on incest, and they had to get a papal dispensation to marry.

the lady-in-waiting to go and speak to the mistress of the palace.

In her memoirs, Pauline describes Marie's arrival. It was clearly a fond memory, and it is worth quoting[38] her at length.

> One day I was sitting quietly in my boudoir, enjoying a book, when my maid came in with an album in her hand. I asked her what she wished to show me; she answered:
>
> "There is a young woman upstairs who has begged me to ask your Highness to look at the sketches in this book; they are designs for dresses, and are the work of her husband. He is extremely anxious to make a gown for you, no matter at what price, if you will allow him to do so."
>
> "What is this man's name?" I inquired.
>
> "His name is Worth, and he is an Englishman."
>
> "An Englishman who dares to claim that he can make women's dresses in Paris! What a strange idea!", I cried. "I want nothing to do with him."
>
> "Nevertheless your Highness would do well to glance at these sketches," said my maid. "To my mind they are very charming."
>
> "Oh, well," said I, impatiently, "let me have a look at them, but I doubt whether your Englishman's designs are at all likely to

---

[38] This English text is taken from the 1922 translation of the memoirs, entitled *My Years in Paris*. I have adapted it slightly because the French version is more detailed. The English translator seems to have edited the text.

appeal to me."

I opened the album, and to my surprise saw the sketch of a fascinating gown on the first page, of an exquisite one on the next.

"Here is an artist," I thought to myself. To the maid I said:

"Bring this Englishwoman to see me."

"She is pure French," said the maid. "There is nothing English about her."

After a few minutes, Madame Worth made her appearance. She was a timid, modest woman who blushed when she spoke ...

Marie was certainly wearing one of her husband's finest day dresses, an outfit designed to impress without getting above its station. Pauline would have noted this, and been re-assured by its almost effortless elegance – Worth's trademark.

While Pauline flicked through the album, Marie explained that her husband had been the head of dressmaking at La Maison Gagelin (a name that would certainly have impressed Pauline) and had now set up in business independently. As Marie spoke, she must have noticed that Charles's designs were working their spell. She realized that now was the time to leap into the breach. After years dealing with Paris's chicest women, Marie knew that even the wealthiest of them loved a discount. Summoning all her courage, she tempted Pauline with the irresistible offer that she and Charles had concocted: they were so keen to count the *Prinzessin* amongst their clients that if she would order a dress from them, she could name her own price.

The ruse worked. Pauline immediately declared that she wanted one morning gown and one evening dress, and that she would pay 300 francs apiece for them.

This was a hundred days' wages for a seamstress. It might sound a lot, but at that time it was a cheap price to pay for made-to-measure garments that used several metres of highly expensive fabric and employed a whole team of workers. Just a few months later, once Worth et Bobergh was prospering, an evening dress would cost almost ten times more.

Pauline stipulated that her evening dress should be ready by the weekend, and that she would undergo only a single fitting. She sugar-coated her demands by adding that she intended to wear it at the next imperial ball on the following Wednesday. In her memoirs she recalled that, hearing this, Marie 'could not contain her joy.'

ꟽꟽꟽ

It is easy to imagine Charles waiting back at the rue de la Paix, anxiously biting his nails, not even sure that Marie would have gained entrance to the Embassy, let alone spoken in person to the famous Pauline von Metternich. Surely the best he could realistically hope for was that Marie had been allowed to leave the catalogue with a servant, in return for a promise that it would be looked at as soon as possible – meaning most likely 'Danke, aber nein danke.'

And then, in breezed Marie with the news that one of Paris's most famous ladies wanted to be dressed in a Worth creation at the very next Tuileries ball. It was the fashion equivalent of an Oscar nomination. A dream on the verge of coming true.

No doubt after much leaping, cheering and hugging (within the boundaries of 19th-century Anglo-French decorum, of course), Charles and his seamstresses got to work. Speed and creativity were of the essence.

After little more than a day's cutting and sewing, Charles sent two dresses, as yet untrimmed, to the Hôtel de Rothelin Charelais. The Worth creative team had been working according to measurements provided by the Embassy, and they must have been accurate because Pauline needed only the single fitting that she had demanded. She was highly impressed. As she remembered, 'It was usual to try on five or six times at other places.' It is unclear from Pauline von Metternich's memoirs whether Charles himself supervised this fitting, but it is very likely. Working against the clock, and with both the Princess's and the Worths' Parisian reputation at stake, nothing less than complete perfection could be contemplated.

After the fitting, the dresses were taken back to the rue de la Paix to be finished. A couple of days later, both outfits were ready. The evening dress was made of white[39] tulle with what Pauline described as 'tiny silver discs' (sequins). To this background Charles had added trimmings that Pauline called 'crimson-hearted daisies that nestled amongst little tufts of feathery grass.' She gushed about it that: 'I have never seen a more beautiful gown, or one that fitted more beautifully.'

Everything was ready for the imperial ball the following Wednesday.

---

[39] At Napoléon III and Eugénie's court the ladies wore white to imperial balls, just as Napoléon I's female courtiers had done. White was considered the classical ideal, echoing the marble of Greek and Roman statues.

7 THE WORTHS GO TO THE BALL

By the winter season of 1859-1860 the weekly balls at the Tuileries palace had become the showpieces of Napoléon III and Eugénie's public life. It was *de rigueur* to be amongst the 5,000 or so guests. Whole families of social climbers would mingle with old aristocrats and new industrial moguls. Foreign businesspeople, often given a ticket as a favour by their ambassadors, would schmooze and stare. Every diplomat in Paris, and every government minister who was not visiting a factory in Lyon or negotiating a treaty in Rome, would be present to see the imperial couple make their appearance.

Wednesdays were the nights when the *crème de la crème* of Paris had to be wildly overdressed. The men were usually in formal evening suits or uniform and medals – standard, repetitive garb – but for the ladies, it was out of the question to wear a gown that had been seen in public before. Getting noticed was the name of the game.

Noticing people was pretty well the sole highlight of these evenings for the Empress Eugénie. Here she was in her role as Napoleon's trophy wife, to be ogled at. She was keenly aware that when she took the floor to open the dancing, ten thousand eyes were scrutinizing her, seeking out the slightest stumble or lapse of good taste.

It was like appearing on stage in the biggest theatre in Europe. Which was why Eugénie had taken coaching sessions with France's most famous actress of the time, Mademoiselle Rachel, a member of the *Comédie Française* (and, incidentally one of Napoléon III's former lovers).

Rachel taught Eugénie posture, comportment and stage presence – in short, how to look like the heroine of a classical play by a French tragedian like Racine or Corneille. Accordingly, on big public occasions, Eugénie would maintain a statuesque, imperturbable façade and reacted to a guest only if protocol demanded it, or if she spotted someone who looked truly remarkable.

In Napoléon III's Paris, garnering imperial favour was everyone's goal. The French Revolution had apparently been forgotten, and these balls rekindled the days when every courtier's dream was to attract a glance or a word from King Louis XIV as he marched along the corridors of the Palais de Versailles from his dinner to his commode.

ϖϖϖ

On that winter Wednesday in early 1860, Charles and Marie Worth went to bed early, but if they had gone to brave the cold in the rue de Rivoli, they would have seen the carriages lining up to enter the Tuileries Palace courtyard. They would probably have caught a glimpse of the *Prinzessin* shivering in the Austrian ambassador's coach.

Inside the Palace, guests gathered in the Salle des Maréchaux – the marshals' room – an enormous function hall decorated in white and gilt, and lit by huge hanging crystal chandeliers. Taking up most of one wall was the imperial dais which was swathed in red velvet and framed by four vast semi-naked caryatids[40]. It was a theatre stage waiting for the First Couple's grand entrance.

Around the dais there was seating for the most honoured guests. In the centre sat the imperial family circle: chief amongst these was Napoléon III's cousin Mathilde, who had got into the habit of playing a hypocritical game with Eugénie – respectful to her face, bitchy behind her back. Then there was Lucien Murat, son of the original Napoléon Bonaparte's sister Caroline and Joachim Murat, one of the generals at Waterloo. Lucien's son was an army colonel who had fought at the recent battles of Magenta and Solferino – a national hero to be shown off at the Tuileries.

To the left of the imperial dais sat Eugénie's entourage of ladies-in-waiting – the impeccably dressed wives and daughters of high-ranking French and Spanish families, some of them appointed by Napoléon to keep an eye on his wife. And to the right sat the diplomatic contingent, amongst them Pauline von Metternich.

Out in the non-VIP area of the room, the crush was oppressive, largely because the average woman took up as much space as a two-seater sofa in her absurdly bulky crinoline. A pair of ladies brushing against each other risked staying joined for life if their ribbons became entangled. Fans flapped, long feathers tickled noses, and men's sword scabbards threatened to rip the tulle that most ball gowns were made of.

At nine on the dot a palace official called out 'L'Empereur!' and into this glittering, chattering scene the imperial couple emerged. The Emperor – who had

---

[40] Statues that seem to be holding up a balcony, roof or other architectural structure.

genuine battle experience, albeit against his own countrymen – was wearing a general's uniform with gold epaulettes, and his waxed moustache was probably the shiniest thing in the room. Eugénie was in shimmering white, accessorized with a cascade of diamonds.

The first guests to be greeted by the imperial couple were always the ambassadors and their wives, and Pauline von Metternich's gown caught Eugénie's jaded eye. 'Hardly had the Empress entered the Throne Room,' Pauline remembered, 'than she immediately noticed my dress, recognizing at a glance that a master had been at work.'
'Your dress is lovely,' Eugénie told Pauline. 'It is perfectly charming. Who made it?'
'An Englishman, Madame,' Pauline replied, 'a new star that has suddenly risen in the firmament of fashion.' (Surely Pauline re-wrote her dialogue for her memoirs here, unless she had prepared a speech for the occasion.)
'Well, the new star must be provided with satellites,' Eugénie reportedly said, 'so will you kindly ask him to come and see me tomorrow at ten o'clock?'
Pauline replied that she would be delighted to do so, and must have felt very proud of herself. Not only had she impressed the Empress, she had achieved what she and Marie Worth had hoped for. In her autobiography Pauline sportingly quips: 'I was done for; no dress for three hundred francs ever again saw the light of day.'

ღღღ

Next morning she sent word to the rue de la Paix that her mission was accomplished, and the Worths must have celebrated even more riotously. This was the chance of a lifetime, the first step of a marble staircase that could take them to the heights of dizzying wealth, maybe even on to the guest list at the Tuileries.

Having dealt with the imperial staff in the past, the Worths knew about the etiquette surrounding a tradesman's visit to the Palace. Marie, timid by nature, would have insisted that Charles obey the rules to the letter so as not to shock his prospective new client – this was the tactic they had adopted every day when they were employed at La Maison Gagelin. However, Charles decided that it was time to make his mark. He would play the maverick artist. If he was, as Pauline von Metternich said, a rising star in the dressmaking world, he needed to act the part. He could not afford to shrink back into the subservient role of the fabric shop salesman or the passive female dressmaker.

So Charles resolved to take risks.

First of all, he refused to change into the formal garb that was usually required of a man who had been granted an audience at the palace with the Empress. Protocol demanded black tails and a white tie, with golden buttons on the shirt cuffs. But Charles Worth decided to go along to the Tuileries dressed in his ordinary (albeit chic) working outfit – a smart but non-formal frock coat. This would be the equivalent today of putting on a jacket and tie instead of a morning suit[41].

Charles had already begun defying conventional class distinctions in a different way. These days we are used to seeing portraits of men of that period with ample facial hair. Napoléon III, the leader of French male fashion,

---

[41] Some sources suggest that Charles Worth had no time to buy a court costume before going to the palace, but this is hardly credible. Working in the fashion business, he could have got himself fitted out in no time at all.

always wore a moustache and goatee, and we have hardly ever glimpsed a square inch of Monet's or Rodin's complexion. A photo from the early 1860s shows Charles Worth sporting an impressively drooping Mexican-bandit moustache, but as Jean-Philippe Worth noted when describing his father's first visit to the Tuileries: 'In the middle of the 19th century a judge or a notary might adorn his upper lip, but the mere head of a commercial establishment, never!' It would have been tempting to make a good impression at the Tuileries by being clean-shaven, but Charles decided to flaunt his luscious moustache.

ϖϖϖ

The unconventional Englishman arrived at the Palace shortly before ten o'clock and was taken up a marble staircase to a waiting room at the entrance to the Empress's private apartments. An usher was sent to tell the ladies-in-waiting that Monsieur Worth was in attendance.

Charles was then escorted through the Empress's remarkable blue, pink and green *salons* (each one decorated with furniture, curtains and rugs of the appropriate colour) and into her dressing room, a large area with almost no furniture except wall mirrors – Eugénie needed plenty of space to don her outfits.

At one end of the dressing room was a lift shaft. The Empress's enormous collection of clothes was stored on the floor above. The writer Maxime du Camp claimed to have seen Eugénie's wardrobe. There, he said, 'dresses were permanently displayed on life-size mannequins, so as not to crease.' The outfit required by the Empress for any occasion was sent down in the lift, on its wickerwork dummy, complete with dress, cloak and even underwear.

In this way, Eugénie could walk around the mannequin, examining it from all angles and judging how she was going to look. Then she would send the garments back upstairs, ordering adjustments through a speaking tube to the ladies above. Dressing the Empress was an industrial process.

Many of these outfits had never been worn before. Eugénie would order large quantities of dresses and then wear each one in public only once. Clothes sported by the Empress at some imperial occasion would then be given away to her friends, family and favourites at a twice-yearly ceremony[42]. Charles Worth certainly knew this and was aware that in a single season of official events, she might need a hundred unique outfits. The potential earnings for her dressmakers were stupendous.

He had little time to dwell on the future before the punctual Eugénie arrived to greet him. She was polite, although her manner was inevitably condescending – or as Jean-Philippe subtly expressed it, she was 'a little spoiled by the warm sunshine of life.'

Physically, Charles noted, the Empress was very beautiful when seen close up. Many accounts of that time give gushing accounts of Eugénie's effect on people when they first met her. Jean-Philippe Worth describes his own encounter with religious fervour: 'Had the Virgin Mary suddenly smiled at me, I could not have been more awed. Indeed, so far as appearance was concerned, she was not without a certain divinity. When

---

[42] Eugénie's lady-in-waiting Amélie Carette reported in her memoirs that some of the recipients would make healthy profits selling the imperial outfits to America, where companies had been set up to rent out the Empress's dresses for an evening. Seamstresses would temporarily adjust the gowns to the client's size.

she smiled her expression was soft and winning, her lips were all the more scarlet for the whiteness of her magnificent teeth, and her hair was dark red with a hint of gold.'

In her memoirs, Pauline von Metternich confesses that she was just as spellbound:

> Even greater than [Eugénie's] beauty was the incomparable grace of every movement – it would have been possible to paint her in any and every position into which she naturally fell [...] I must frankly own that I was quite taken aback by the impression produced on me by this beautiful woman, whose good taste had also made her the arbiter of fashion.

At this first private interview, Charles fought the temptation to fall under the Empress's spell. He forced himself to cast a professional eye over her, and apparently succeeded, because he later described to his son Jean-Philippe his impression that the happiness of Eugénie's early years in Paris seemed to have waned. As a young bride, her favourite colour had been sky blue, he said: now it was pearl grey. But she showed natural grace, and Charles thought that her red-golden hair cried out to be matched by vividly-coloured fabrics.

He was surprised to see that she was simply dressed – this was her custom when she was at home, as a comfortable contrast to the heavy, awkward outfits she had to wear in public.

The Empress told Charles that she had seen his gowns at (at least) one of her *soirées* and asked how he would dress her if he were given the opportunity. Charles sensed that it was time to seize the moment.

He knew that the Empress wanted more than anything else to make an impression, to silence her critics with sheer magnificence. She was also known for her strong personal taste where aesthetics were concerned. For her variously-coloured *salons* she had chosen an unconventional mix of antique furniture (the royal norm) and modern pieces that were at the cutting edge of design. Eugénie was using the Palace itself to express her personality. Her clothes needed to do the same.

Charles was conscious that he too had to prove his individuality, so he made some deliberately bold suggestions about shapes and colours. However, initially the Empress resisted. He later told his son Jean-Philippe that she was 'belligerently *réfractaire*' (unyielding). Nevertheless – the point of his visit – she did put in an order for one outfit, and agreed to give him some leeway in the design. She wanted him to surprise her, she said.

He was told that he would receive the Empress's measurements from one of her staff. Then, as suddenly as it had begun, the audience was at an end, and Charles was escorted back through the blue, pink and green *salons* and out into the street.

It was a modest start, a single order. But Eugénie's patronage was what Jean-Philippe Worth called 'the ultimate accolade of success.'

It was also a test, a sort of entrance exam to the promised land of wealth and reputation, and Charles was determined to pass it.

ʊʊʊ

In an interview published in *Le Figaro* in 1889, Charles describes how he decided to take a risk: 'The first of my creations that I submitted to the Empress was a town gown in grey taffeta, decorated with black velvet ribbons, a matching skirt and jacket. At that time it was new, even if it has now become commonplace.'

We can be sure that Charles and his team threw everything into the project – their finest woven silk taffeta, their most sultry black velvet, their minutest stitching. The Empress was going to get literally the best cloth and the best workmanship (or workwomanship – the sewing was done by female fingers) available in France, put together by a man with a natural eye for the cut of a dress and the way fabrics hung and moved when worn.

Charles took the outfit to the Tuileries – we are not sure exactly when, but it was presumably very soon after the initial interview, as proof of his team's reliability. And, as he remembered it, 'the Empress admired it greatly.'

But there was a problem.

'Mr Worth, I would not like to show myself in public wearing such a new style. I must wait until it has been worn by someone else. In my position, I must not create fashion, I must content myself with following it.'

This must have come as a crushing disappointment to Charles. Everyone in the creative industries knows the 'thanks but no thanks' rejection, or, even worse, 'you're a genius but not our kind of genius.'

Nevertheless, there was hope: Worth's client Mélanie de Pourtalès lived about a kilometre away from the Tuileries, in a mansion in the rue Tronchet, just the other side of La Madeleine. Perhaps Charles rushed there immediately, with an explanatory note from Eugénie. In any case, the upshot was that, as Charles told *Le Figaro*, 'the Comtesse de Pourtalès took the outfit.' After some adjustments she wore it, maybe on a stroll along the boulevard Haussmann which was at the end of her street, and the Worths were left to wait, praying that the fashion for matching skirt and jacket would catch on.

It was all horribly frustrating. The game-changing order from the Empress had been so near and yet so far.

Mélanie de Pourtalès's outing in her new ensemble must have caught the eye of Paris's smart set and started a fashion, because as Charles tells it: 'Only six months later, I made one exactly similar for the Empress, who wore it to the races at Vincennes[43].'

In fact, we know that Eugénie was wearing other Worth creations before those six months were up. By the summer of 1860, Charles received confirmation that he had earned Eugénie's full trust: Worth et Bobergh was ordered to outfit the Empress for a whole season. She changed clothes five or six times a day, and needed morning wear, lunch attire, afternoon dresses and evening gowns. Each outfit, of course, to be worn only once in public.

This was the order that Charles and Marie had dreamt about. It was like an architect being commissioned to build a whole new town. The only requirement was that each individually designed house, as it was unveiled, should make the residents of the town swoon with envy and admiration.

Just a few months earlier, Charles Worth had been a relatively obscure dressmaker with a smattering of in-the-know clients. He had left the famous firm, Gagelin, that had 'created' him, and was struggling to turn a profit in a street, the rue de la Paix, which did not seem

---

[43] The race course east of Paris, near the château of the same name. However, the course was not built until 1863 which suggests that Charles's memory was playing tricks on him.

particularly well chosen because it was outside the garment district. A neutral observer might have said that his decisions lacked discernment. Now he was the man who – and this is no exaggeration – had been given the responsibility of dressing the most glamorous woman in Europe.

At the age of 35, Charles could look back on almost 25 years of tireless preparation for this moment. He also knew that he was lucky to have beside him Marie, the woman who had believed in his creativity from the start, and who had overcome her natural modesty to become his living *mannequin*, even when she was pregnant and in physical pain inside his brutally tight bodices. Now, by talking her way into the Austrian Embassy, she had secured his place in the public spotlight and launched their business on a course for stratospheric success.

Naturally, as soon as it became known that Worth was dressmaker to the Empress, high-society orders began to flood in.

ღღღ

By 1860, Napoléon III's Second Empire had become an era of shameless entrepreneurship and capitalism. If cash was there to be taken, you took it. It you had it, you spent it – lavishly and publicly. And the rich were only too willing to spend their money *chez* Worth.

Paris had originally been dubbed the *ville lumière* (city of light) because of the philosophical enlightenment in the 18th century. Now Baron Haussmann was punching his modern boulevards through central Paris, turning it into a literally brightly-lit city, while at the crossroads of several of these new streets, Charles Garnier was building an opera house with more decoration than an Empress's wedding cake. The city's new streetlights were shining down on a circus of ostentation.

In this climate, more than ever, rich women in Paris were obliged to dress up. Shabbiness did not get you invited to receptions and balls at the Tuileries, or to Napoléon III's week-long house-parties at the Château de Compiègne, north of Paris, and the Château de Fontainebleau to the south. And, as we saw earlier, it was forbidden for ladies to wear the same outfit to two imperial events, so that every occasion was a première for every single dress.

At the height of Worth's career, a good proportion of the 2,500 or so female guests at the four imperial balls per winter season wanted to be dressed by him. He would also be called upon to outfit many of the 200 ladies at Eugénie's Monday parties in her blue *salon*. This meant, say, 1,000 dresses per ball and 100 per Monday party – all to be ready on the same nights. It was insanely stressful, but fantastically lucrative.

Charles's outfits also became obligatory evening wear outside imperial venues.

Soon after Eugénie's first appearance in a Worth creation, Charles was summoned by Napoléon III's cousin Mathilde, who needed outfits to impress the regulars at her *salons* in the Parisian mansion that her cousin Napoléon I had given her.

Charles was also invited to call on the Russian-born Duchess Sophie de Morny, the wife of Napoléon III's half-brother Charles de Morny (both were sons, by different fathers, of Hortense de Beauharnais, the daughter of Napoléon Bonaparte's Joséphine). The Mornys were part of the imperial entourage, and held frequent *soirées* at their home, the Hôtel de Lassay, a palace that is currently the official residence of the President of the French *Assemblée Nationale*. It lies just across the river from the Tuileries and next to the Palais

Bourbon (the seat of the *Assemblée Nationale*).

Less welcome but equally profitably, the most notorious of Paris's *demi-mondaines* (a polite word for high-class prostitutes) began to order from Worth et Bobergh. Like everyone else in Paris under the Second Empire, the Worths did not inquire about the source of the money they received. The boundary between moral and immoral earnings was irreparably blurred. These loose women had money to burn and could afford the most expensive dresses Charles could create. Amongst them was La Païva, the Russian-born mistress of a Prussian count, owner of a small palace at number 25 avenue des Champs-Elysées. Another was the actress and courtesan Elise Musard, known as Madame Musard. A 'favourite' of the serial philanderer King William III of Holland, she would later become rich enough to leave Paris and settle in a villa on Lake Como. Meanwhile, she spent her Dutch income in the rue de la Paix.

ཙཙཙ

Charles Worth's star rose so quickly that all these rich ladies except Eugénie herself were soon going along to Worth et Bobergh for their fittings instead of demanding that he come to their homes.[44] Here, Marie Worth came into her own. She was the social face of the business, a Eugénie to her husband's Napoléon III. She often had to make conversation (while wearing one of Charles's creations, of course) as the esteemed visitors waited for their audience with the Great Man.

On arriving in the courtyard of 7 rue de la Paix,

---

[44] There is a story, perhaps apocryphal, about one princess who instructed Charles to go to her, but who received the reply that he was 'too busy with the princesses who had come to him.'

customers would be helped down from their carriages by smartly-dressed young commissionaires, some of whom affected English accents, and then escorted up a red-carpeted staircase to the showrooms. The public spaces were fitted out to resemble the reception rooms of an *haute bourgeoisie* home. Rugs and wallpapers were fashionably patterned. Plush armchairs, chandeliers, and freshly cut flowers were everywhere. The snootiest clients were meant to feel *chez eux*.

In 1863, another Charles – Dickens – gave a description of clients arriving at the rue de la Paix. England's most famous novelist had not witnessed Worth in action himself: he was translating from a book, *La Nouvelle Babylone – lettres d'un provincial en tournée à Paris, (New Babylon – Letters from a Provincial on Tour in Paris)*, published the previous year by a writer called Eugène Pelletan.[45] Dickens was no doubt attracted to Pelletan's story because of the rare spectacle of an Englishman causing such a splash in Paris. Here is an excerpt from the English translation:

> Whenever there is a ball at court, or at the Hôtel de Ville, or an evening party or ceremony at the Palais Royal or the Luxembourg, at about ten o'clock you will see a long file of carriages drawn up before the house of the foreign ladies' tailor, with their melancholy coachmen buried in their wraps. Their mistresses mount the staircase of the Temple de la Toilette. As they enter, they each receive a ticket in the order of their arrival, and are shown into a waiting-room.

---

[45] Dickens published the text in his diary in magazine form, *All The Year Round*. This is from volume 9.

As they can only appear one by one in the presence of the Pontiff of the Skirt, the last-comers have sometimes to wait a long while [...] A buffet, liberally supplied, offers the consolation of meats and pastry. The ethereal *petites maîtresses* of the Paris saloons lay in a stock of strength for the polka, by eating *pâté de foie gras* at discretion, and washing it down with Malmsey Madeira.

Sudden success forced the Worths to adapt very quickly. They created extra showrooms and workshops. Thanks to their enhanced reputation, they were able to attract an army of new seamstresses and models – including some cutters from England – and Charles hired experienced personal assistants to help at fittings, almost all of them female. (For more details about the workers in the Parisian fashion business, see chapter 10.)

The original first-floor premises at the rue de la Paix were soon too cramped to house the Worth family as well as receiving customers and creating garments. They rented the second floor, and moved their private apartments upstairs, overlooking the courtyard.

Most of these changes began within a matter of weeks after Eugénie's first order. The expansion was hectic but smooth, because Charles and Marie were seizing an opportunity that they had dreamt about for years – they were applying what we would today call their business plan.

The market for expensive women's clothes was already huge when Charles first went to see Eugénie. And the plan was to make it even huger, not just by attracting new clients but also by modernizing working practices in the industry.

As we saw earlier, the old method of renewing a high-society lady's wardrobe involved a lot of what the French delicately call *'retouches'*. Seamstresses added new touches to old dresses or, in the best of cases, made new versions of old designs. Such parsimony was now to become a thing of the past. According to the Worth philosophy, if a woman wanted to shine in Napoléon and Eugénie's Paris, every outfit had to be entirely new, styled by Charles Worth and ridiculously expensive, because Worth was the best in the business and quality comes at a price.

In short, the Englishman and his French wife were setting out on a mission to revolutionize the world of Parisian fashion.

8 THE BIRTH OF FRENCH *HAUTE COUTURE*

The transformations now instigated at number 7 rue de la Paix were destined to influence the fashion industry right up until the present day. Quite simply, without Worth, clothing brands like Chanel, Dior, Lagerfeld and McQueen might not have existed. Or if they had been created, the individuals of that name would probably have remained faceless designers at one end of an industrial production line.

All the basics of what we now call *haute couture* (a term that first came into common use in the 1880s) were put in place at Worth et Bobergh.

Marie had been the first full-time live *mannequin*, and in their new roomy premises the Worths had the space to go one further, and create a full fashion show with a team of models. After passing through three showrooms hung with lengths of fabric – black and white silks, then coloured silks, followed by velvets – clients were ushered into a large showroom lined with mirrors, where young female employees were on hand to try on any of Charles's new creations that a customer wanted to see 'in action'. Ladies could sit and admire the gowns as the models promenaded them up and down the showroom. The catwalk was born.

Olivia Worth van Hoegaerden showed me a Pathé newsreel filmed at the rue de la Paix in the 1930s. In black and white, we see smiling models parading along the balconies, which are emblazoned with large metal letters: WORTH.

There is also a long shot down the corridor that linked all the rooms at the front of the building. Models, with their short bob haircuts, perform what has now become the characteristic catwalk step – one foot placed directly in front of the other – and then stop in front of seated clients to give them a twirl of a coat or dress. A row of chic ladies wearing mink wraps and bell-shaped 1930s hats, seated on what look like gilt Napoléon III armchairs, admire a whole season's autumn-winter collection.

Similar scenes must have taken place sixty-odd years earlier in the same premises, and they have been repeated at every Paris Fashion Week since.

Charles Worth even invented a sort of fantasy show for his customers. If a lady was tempted by any of the gowns worn by the models, she could then go into his *Salon des Lumières* and try on the dress herself, in a room that was lit to resemble a ballroom *soirée*. It was like a modern virtual-reality experience.

ϖϖϖ

A key innovation introduced at 7 rue de la Paix was the sense that you, *la cliente* (or the man who was paying for all this, because in the 1860s women still had no right to money of their own), were unbelievably privileged to be accepted as a customer. Being admitted into Charles Worth's presence meant that you possessed some undefinable quality (apart from your wealth) that his clothes could enhance, confirming your rightful place amongst the élite at the heart of Europe's most glittering social scene.

To achieve this, Charles treated his favourite clients like confidantes. Pauline von Metternich remembered him acting this way with her: 'He would sometimes say "Madame is quite a decent sort of woman, but she has no more brains than a linnet. She thinks that beautiful clothes are in themselves quite sufficient to make a woman look distinguished. She doesn't realize that it is perfectly impossible to disguise the fact that she is middle-class from top to toe, no matter how exquisitely she may be dressed by me."'

The subtext was, of course, 'You, *ma chère* Pauline, are different – you're pure class. You're the kind of client I *really* want, even if I'm forced to cater for lesser beings.' He probably said it to all the ladies.

Charles had developed a fully-fledged character: the dandyish, amusingly opinionated Englishman in Paris. When he spoke English, the remnants of his Lincolnshire burr might have betrayed his humble origins to a snobbish Londoner, but Americans didn't notice this. And when he spoke French, even to the haughtiest *Parisienne*, he was classless, with a soft, appealing accent that they identified simply as *'anglais'*. As a typical Brit, he almost certainly couldn't pronounce the guttural French R, so that he would have made 'soir' (evening) sound like 'soie' (silk), but by now he could converse confidently in French, and knew how to win over the most cynical client with a well-crafted Gallic compliment.

Charles went further, and morphed into the archetypal 19th-century Parisian creative genius. According to a contemporary of his, a writer and philosopher called Hippolyte Taine, Charles was keen for everyone to know it: 'I have Delacroix's sense of colour,' Worth is quoted as saying, 'and I compose. A *toilette*[46] is as good as a painting.'

This frequently cited quotation should be taken with a pinch of salt. It comes from Taine's 1867 novel *Notes sur Paris*, which was cruelly satirical. His narrator meets an unnamed character who is clearly meant to be Worth and whom he obviously hates. The arrogant dressmaker claims that his clients, like a portraitist's subjects, have to be at his beck and call, whatever their social rank. They must obey him precisely because he is *un artiste*: 'In all artists there is a bit of Napoléon,' he says. 'Art is God and the bourgeois are there to take our orders.'

However, in attributing these opinions to Charles Worth, Taine may well have been going only one satirical step beyond reality, because the view of clothes as art was perfectly in tune with the times. Another Charles, the poet Baudelaire, the voice of France's aesthetic movement, wrote with total sincerity in 1863 that: 'For the artist, woman is not only the female of the man. Rather she is a divinity, a guiding star, presiding over every creation of the male brain. [...] Everything that adorns a woman, everything that serves to show off her beauty, is part of herself, [...] not only in her bearing and in the way she moves and walks, but also in the muslins, the gauzes, the vast iridescent cloud of material in which she envelops herself.'[47] To modern ears this may sound horrifically patronizing, but it was the philosophy of the

---

[46] A reminder: this was not a reference to graffiti in a toilet, of course: again, *toilette* is the French term for an outfit of clothes.
[47] Quoted from *Le Peintre de la vie moderne* (*The Painter of Modern Life*), published as a series of essays on beauty in the newspaper *Le Figaro*. Baudelaire added that woman 'is a kind of idol, stupid maybe but dazzling.' Not exactly a feminist.

period amongst Paris's chattering classes, and whether Charles Worth really claimed to be Delacroix or not, he exploited the clothes-as-art attitude to great effect.

The fitting room was his artist's studio. He would give a running commentary as he and his assistants draped lengths of cloth around his bewitched female subject. The previously quoted report by Eugène Pelletan via Charles Dickens contains a vivid description of Worth's painterly technique. Pelletan punctuated his description with irony, but he could not hide his admiration for the skill with which Worth carried off his act:

> It must be avowed that this *Anglais* has created a novel art – the art of squeezing in a woman at the waist, with a precision hitherto unknown. He possesses the inspiration of handling the scissors [...] He knows to a thread the exact point where the stuff ought to fit tight, and where it ought to float loosely. At first sight he distinguishes, in the contexture of a lady, what ought to be displayed and what concealed. [...]
>
> From time to time he draws back, in order to judge better of his work from a distance; he looks through his hand, closed into the shape of an eye-glass, and resumes with inspired fingers the modelling of the drapery on the person of the patient.
>
> Sometimes he plants a flower here, and tries a bow of ribbon at its side, to test the general harmony of the *toilette* ; meanwhile, the modern Eve, in process of formation, resigned and motionless, silently allows her moulder to accomplish his

creation. At last, when he has handled the taffeta like clay, and arranged it according to his beau ideal, he goes and takes his place, with his head thrown back, on a sofa at the further end of the room, whence he commands the manoeuvre with a wand of office.

"To the right, Madame!" The client performs a quarter of a revolution.

"To the left!" The patient turns in the opposite direction.

"In front!" Madame faces the artist.

"Behind!" She turns her back.

When all is over, he dismisses her with a lordly gesture: "That will do, Madame."

One of Worth's most fashionable clients, Comtesse de Mercy-Argenteau, a pianist, composer, and mistress of Napoléon III, confirms that this was Charles's usual *modus operandi*. In her memoirs, she recalls:

> Worth was very amusing, and his vogue came quite as much from his personality as from his talent as a dressmaker. When I wanted an important *toilette* for a Court ball I had to call several times. He would first look at me for a long time without speaking, then, in an inspired and faraway voice: "light gauze ... pearl grey ... roses and leaves ... a trail of lace ..." and he would disappear. If he decided that I was to wear blue or green I had to do as I was told. He was a tyrant, but we all adored him.

Émile Zola satirizes Charles's artistic pose in his novel *La Curée*[48]. He describes a character called Worms (a thinly disguised Charles Worth) gazing at a woman: 'The master was absorbed in the spectacle of his client like Leonardo da Vinci before Mona Lisa.' Sometimes, though, according to Zola: 'Inspiration came reluctantly. The illustrious Worms summoned it in vain, concentrating his faculties with no reward. He twisted his eyebrows, turned deep red, took his poor head in his hands and, defeated, threw himself into an armchair. "No," he would murmur in a doleful voice, "not today, the well is dry." '

Even Pauline von Metternich occasionally found Worth's performance comic. In her memoirs she wrote about the 'absurd little airs which he gave himself, to say nothing of the rather overbearing attitude he was pleased to assume when it was a question of creating a *toilette à sensation*.' But she recognized his 'unerring instinct where women were concerned.'

Pauline illustrates how well Charles had established his persona (and, incidentally, she reminds us how essential she was to his success. She is not exactly modest). It is interesting to quote the passage at length:

> Worth composed *toilettes* that were really dazzling, but he had a way of altering certain little details up to the very last moment. He would change this, and that, sometimes declaring that even one's hair was to be

---

[48] The title is usually translated as *The Kill*, though *'curée'* means booty, referring to the illicit profits earned by speculators in Napoléon III's Second Empire. See chapter 13 for a fuller account of Zola's opinion of Charles Worth.

dressed in an entirely different way; insisting, in fact, on those finishing touches which he, the creator and artist, held to be indispensable.

On one occasion when we had all met at the Rue de la Paix to try on our dresses for the fancy ball that was to take place that very night at the Tuileries, we were told that Worth had a bad headache and had retired to his own apartments. We were quite desperate. What was to be done? No one had the faintest idea how the costumes were to be worn. The young women assistants stood round us like so many logs, unable to supply any information whatsoever. The workwomen [seamstresses] were no better. Skirts, sleeves, bodices had all been made by different people in separate workrooms. What on earth were we to do?

I finally took my courage in both hands and determined to confront the lion in his den. Climbing up to his private apartment, which was situated on the second floor, looking on to the courtyard, I literally burst into his room, where I found him lying on a sofa with bandages tied round his head and over his eyes. I told him he really must pull himself together and make an effort to see us, that he owed it to me not to leave us in the lurch, that he owed it still more to the Empress, who had invited us to the ball. At last he gave his consent. In a voice that was scarcely audible he murmured, "Put on your costumes and come up here."

We hastened to do so, and one by one he inspected us all. The premiere [Worth's chief seamstress] stood by his side, whispering the name of each woman as her turn came round.

Lifting the bandage from his eyes he carefully examined the unfortunate creature who stood before him, muttering at intervals: "Hideous!" "Ridiculous!" "Appalling!" We were quite desperate. At last I had a brain-wave; a great idea — great as the universe itself — flashed into my mind.

"Monsieur Worth," I cried, "you are signing the death-warrant of your reputation to-day." At these words he leaped off the sofa, tore off his bandages, and marching us downstairs, as though we were his troops and he our general, which as a matter of fact was really the case — "Allons! En avant![49]" he cried. [...] Before an hour had elapsed, everything was in order, and that night at the Tuileries no one would have suspected that there had ever been the slightest hitch.

ʊʊʊ

The most scathing view of Worth's dictatorial manner towards his supposedly gullible customers came from an Englishman, Henry Du Pré Labouchère.

Labouchère was stranded in Paris during the Prussian siege of 1870-71 (of which, more in Chapter 15). From the besieged city he sent out reports to *The Daily News* by

---

[49] "Let's go! Forwards!"

hot-air balloon.[50] In his communiqué of 4 January 1871, Labouchère looks back at the time just before the siege, with a macho scorn for the world of fashion[51]. He doesn't even name Worth, assuming that everyone will recognize his portrait of the famous dressmaker:

> The Raphael of his trade gave himself all the airs of a distinguished artist; he received his clients with vulgar condescension, and they – no matter what their rank – submitted to his insolence in the hope that he would enable them to outshine their rivals. Ambassadors' wives and Court ladies used to go to take tea with the fellow, and dispute the honour of filling his cup or putting sugar into it. I once went into his shop – a sort of drawing-room hung round with dresses; I found him lolling on a chair, his legs crossed before the fire. Around him were a bevy of women, some pretty, some ugly, listening to his observations with the rapt attention of the disciples of a sage. He called them up before him like schoolgirls, and after inspecting them, praised or blamed their dresses. One, a pretty young girl, found favour in his eyes, and he told her that he

---

[50] His despatches were later regrouped into a book called *Diary of a Besieged Resident in Paris*.

[51] It is perhaps no coincidence that, serving later as an MP, Labouchère was the instigator of the 1885 British law that made homosexuality illegal. He proposed a minimum sentence of seven years' hard labour, but was persuaded to lower it to a maximum of two. It was under this law that Oscar Wilde and Alan Turing were later prosecuted. Wilde received the maximum sentence.

must dream and meditate several days over her, in order to find the inspiration to make a gown worthy of her. "Why do you wear these ugly gloves?" he said to another, "never let me see you in gloves of that colour again." She was a very grand lady, but she slipped off her gloves, and put them in her pocket with a guilty look. When there was going to be a ball at Court, ladies used to go down on their knees to him to make them beautiful. For some time he declined to dress any longer the wife of a great Imperial dignitary who had not been sufficiently humble towards him; she came to him in tears, but he was obdurate, and he only consented at last to make a gown for her on condition that she would put it on for the first time in his shop. The Empress, who dealt with him, sent to tell him that if he did not abate his prices, she would leave him. "You cannot," he replied, and in fact she could not, for she stood by him to the last. A morning dress by this artist, worth in reality about £4, cost £30; an evening dress, tawdry with flounces, ribbons, and bad lace could not be had under £70. There are about thirty shops in Paris where, as at this man-milliner's, the goods are not better than elsewhere, but where they cost about ten times their value. They are patronized by fools with more money than wits, and chiefly by foreign fools.

This may give the impression that that people were being duped by fakery on Charles Worth's part. But those who knew him well, like Pauline von Metternich, had to concede that amidst all his posing, Worth was deadly serious about his chosen trade. Pauline probably knew that, despite his apparent vagueness, he kept a detailed record of the dresses that he created for each client, so that he would never repeat a trick.

He also made sure that no two women attending the same social occasion would be wearing exactly the same colour or fabric. And once a design had been executed for a truly exceptional customer like Eugénie or a royal, that pattern was never re-used. What was more, any alterations to the size or style of a dress were free of charge to Charles's high-paying *haute couture* clients. His reputation depended not only on creativity but exclusivity and attention to detail.

ღღღ

To tie in with the notion that both his dresses and his clients were unique, Charles had his name sewn into his garments.

As of around 1865, a machine-embroidered 'Worth & Bobergh 7. Rue de la Paix 7. Paris'[52] was sewn into every garment they made. After 1870, when the partnership was dissolved, Worth's name would appear alone. Today, of course, every *haute couture* house possesses its logo, and in airports all over the world there are teams of customs officers deployed to seize T-shirts displaying badly-sewn crocodiles. But before the 1860s, no one had thought of adding a brand name to a dress

---

[52] In the mid-19th century Paris, street numbers were often given *after* the street name. This was changing, however, and here Worth seems to be covering both bases. After 1870 the labels read more simply, 'Worth 7. Rue de la Paix. Paris'.

to prove its provenance and increase its value.

One of Worth's most fervent fans at the time, a Paris-based American singer known as Madame Moulton, wrote about arriving at the Château de Compiègne for an imperial house party, and immediately getting changed into a green tulle dress trimmed with silver: 'If one could see the waistband, one would read Worth in big letters. I thought it was best to make a good impression at the start.' Madame Moulton knew that it would impress the Empress and her entourage to see Worth's signature prominently displayed on a dress. Charles Worth was the first designer to create this desire to show off a clothing brand.

He was probably one of the first to be counterfeited, too. By the 1870s, dishonest traders in several countries had begun making fake Worth labels and sewing them on to their second-rate garments. In 1879 a certain Miss Carson opened a shop in London selling corsets (which La Maison Worth did not make) under the French-sounding name Worth et Cie[53]. It was a very early example of brand piracy.

ʊʊʊ

Other changes that Charles Worth achieved might seem inconsequential today, but at the time they were often shocking. For example: a lady's calves had been hidden for years, except when stiff crinolines accidentally rode up and exposed the lower regions of her legs – or even more if she sat down too quickly. But the consensus in

---

[53] An abbreviation of 'Compagnie'. At first the Worths tolerated this usurpation, and only sued when Worth et Cie started making dresses too.

1860 was that female calves were, barring accident, taboo. Even women's shoes were usually invisible.

However, this was true only for the social classes who could afford the lengths of material necessary to cover themselves up. The niceties of fashion did not apply to the poor, whose main priority was keeping their essentials warm and dry. And one day, in the street (so the story goes), Charles Worth saw a poor woman hitch up her skirt to keep it out of the dirt.

The aesthetic effect appealed to Charles, so he designed something similar for Marie to try out, with a hemline ten centimetres above the ground, maintaining decency (no view of the calves) while giving just a tantalizing glimpse of ankle boot. In fact, it was a practical idea, because most women were sick of dragging their long skirts through the dust and mud of the streets. Marie wore the outfit for strolls along the boulevards – her open-air catwalk – and once the shocked glances of passers-by had become less frequent, Charles took the idea to Eugénie: a short, above-the-ankle, crinoline dress in a tartan[54] material. He called it a 'walking dress'.

By now he had clearly convinced the Empress that her image was so strong (thanks to him, of course) that she was invulnerable to the criticisms of her petty detractors. She, like him, was now a star. So Eugénie wore the new dress with a tight jacket, a small bonnet and a walking stick, and the style was an immediate hit. In 1863, the artist Eugène Boudin painted Eugénie and her ladies-in-waiting on the seafront at the Normandy resort of Trouville, all wearing these off-the-ground dresses.

---

[54] A wily nod to Eugénie's Celtic heritage.

Worth developed the idea for everyday city wear, producing a 'walking costume', consisting of a jacket and ankle-revealing skirt of the same material. This was again premièred by Eugénie and soon adopted by everyone else. It took two or three years for this brazenness to become commonplace in Paris, and then only during the daytime, but at the time the short(er) skirt was considered such a revolution in women's appearance that it was mentioned in some of Charles Worth's obituaries in 1895 as one of his greatest achievements. An Irish newspaper, *The Leitrim Advertiser*, looked back on his career and stated that: 'He thus suppressed the trailing skirt for street wear – a fashion at once unclean and inconvenient.'

ღღღ

Charles also used Eugénie's patronage to promote the use of modern techniques in cloth design. Industry was creating new colours, new fabrics and cheaper versions of old ones – damasks with increasingly bold woven designs, for example, taffeta using synthetic fibres as well as woven silk, and machine-worked brocades (woven cloth with an embossed design).

Jean-Philippe Worth tells the story of his father's campaign to boost the newly mechanized silk-weaving industry of Lyon.

The city was not a Bonapartist stronghold. It had a fiercely independent reputation. Lyon's silk workers had rioted in the 1830s, demanding better conditions in the new mills that the Industrial Revolution had spawned, and each time thousands of troops had been sent in by King Louis Philippe to quell the uprising. Then in 1848 and 1849 there had been insurrections against the way that the new Republic – of which the future Napoléon III was president – had been set up.

In short, the Emperor saw the *Lyonnais* as unreliable, so he was refusing to support their industries. But Charles Worth adored the woven silk patterns coming out of the region, and he created a dress for Eugénie that was made entirely out of Lyon brocade. Jean-Philippe wrote that:

> The colour was beige and the flower design woven into the fabric was taken from a rare Chinese shawl.
> But when [my father] showed it to Eugénie, she gave it one look and declared flatly, "I shan't wear it, it would make me look like a curtain."
> "But Your Majesty," declared my father, "won't you wear it for the sake of what your patronage would mean to the manufacturers of Lyon?"
> Eugénie smiled ironically. "Why? Because they have been so good to us?" referring sardonically to the opposition of Lyon to herself and the Emperor.
> [Napoléon III was, for once, in Eugénie's dressing room, and Charles turned to him:]
> "Oh Sire, please persuade Her Majesty to wear this dress. There are probably ten or twelve leaders of fashion waiting for me at my shop, and upon my return I shan't be able to get out of my coat before they fly at me, screaming, 'Show us what the Empress chose, show us what the Empress chose.' And as soon as I tell them, they will immediately order dresses of the same material and five minutes later the city of Lyon will know that the Empress has

honoured them by wearing a dress of their newest material."

The Emperor nodded agreement to my father's eloquence and turning to Eugénie said, "Monsieur Worth is right. Wear that dress only once[55], [even] if you don't like it, but at least wear it that once." [...]

So the Empress consented to wear the dress of beige brocade that "looked like a curtain" and Lyon silk became a household word. [...]

Statistics were brought forward to show that when my father persuaded Eugénie to wear the dress "like a curtain" he automatically increased the looms in operation in Lyon from 57,500 to 120,000.

These were not only silk looms. Lyon was also home to a satin-weaving industry, but satin was not commonly used in dresses worn at high-society functions. Charles understood this: he was not happy with the designs on offer, so he badgered Lyon's satin manufacturers to produce richer, finer cloths. They followed his instructions and were soon turning out satins worthy of even an Empress's gowns. With Eugénie's support, Charles was almost single-handedly reviving a whole sector of France's textile industry.

As we have seen before, in the past it had been entirely unheard of for a dressmaker to tell a high-society lady, let alone an Empress, what to wear. Now, thanks to Charles Worth, a pedestal for fashion designers had been erected and the first genius had jumped up on it. Chanel,

---

[55] Had Eugénie's husband not realized that she wore *all* her dresses in public only once?

Saint Laurent, Dior et al would all effectively be standing on his shoulders.

Charles did not stop there. Women's clothes of the 19th century were so all-enveloping that today we may not notice changes that at the time were often considered outrageous. But Worth was also responsible for a whole list of innovations: the dress with no seam at the waistline, so that the bodice rose out of the skirt like the neck of a bottle; bolero jackets (inspired by Eugénie's Spanish origins, of course) as ordinary day wear; transparent wisps of cloth to replace heavy shawls; and the 'tunic dress', consisting of a bodice with a short skirt that overlapped a longer one. For his tunic dresses and jacket-and-skirt combinations, Charles often experimented with contrasting fabrics, putting velvet over lace, lace over silk, and so on – anything to create a new, and yet elegant, effect.

According to Jean-Philippe, his father single-handedly popularized the wearing of spectacular lacework. In the past, women had used it sparingly. Now Charles did more than just add frilly trimmings to a dress. He commissioned copies of old laces and ordered outlandish new patterns that he would copyright for his exclusive use. He would then create outfits around lengths of a unique piece of lace.

He also persuaded Marie to help him change hair fashions. Jean-Philippe Worth tells a story about his father taking a pair of scissors to Marie's fringe. In the early 1860s women wore headbands to keep their locks off their forehead. Charles, though, had seen portraits of women from Napoléon Bonaparte's First Empire, when neo-classicism was the rage and female fashions were far more *au naturel*. Trend-setters like the Empress Joséphine and Juliette Récamier, the young hostess of a Parisian literary *salon*, wore flimsy revealing dresses and let their hair flop down over their forehead in fringes like those we see on Greek and Roman sculptures. There is a well-known portrait of Madame Récamier by François Gérard, painted in 1805, that shows her wearing what looks like a thin nightdress, while gazing out from beneath a charming set of black ringlets.

In fact, these drooping locks were usually hairpieces, and the revealing gowns would have been a step too far for the more prudish 1860s, but Charles Worth liked the look and managed to convince Marie to let him cut her hair short at the front and tease a fringe down towards her eyebrows.

This went entirely against the current fashion, and yet again we have to admire Marie for allowing herself to be used as a guinea pig. Parisian society was bitchy, and *le ridicule* was never far away – as we have seen, even Eugénie was not immune to its attacks. But Marie took the risk, and one evening, when she attended an opera with her new hairstyle, she made the headlines. According to Jean-Philippe Worth, the journalist Émile de Girardin, founder of the popular newspaper *La Presse*, wrote that: 'Pretty Madame Worth appeared last night wearing her hair in a fashion that made her resemble Madame Récamier and which was very much admired.'

Inevitably, news of this revolution reached the Tuileries. At first, Eugénie was horrified to hear that it meant cutting her famous locks, but eventually she gave in, and once the Empress herself had a fringe, every fashionable lady in town felt obliged to sport the Marie Worth look.

9 THE DEADLY CRINOLINE

There was one element of female fashion that Charles Worth was determined to change, but which at first seemed untouchable. This elephant in the fitting room was the crinoline.

These days, the only truly absurd, unwearable clothes that we see are on catwalks or red carpets. We have become accustomed to watching footage from Paris Fashion Week in which some underfed model risks serious injury while stumbling along on stilt-high heels, or squints through a headdress as big as a fridge. We watch the arrivals at New York's Met Ball wrapped up like mummies in cellophane, needing a team of assistants to help them into the ballroom. And at awards ceremonies we see pop stars dressed in raw meat.

But all that is just for the cameras, for the fifteen seconds of fame. In the 1860s, on the other hand, absurdity was part of everyday life for any woman who wanted to be fashionable.

Not only did these society ladies sometimes break ribs and rupture organs to squeeze into minute corsets, they also 'had to' wear the crinoline, a metal-and-fabric structure hidden underneath their skirt that could measure two metres across, and which meant that they could not sit on a chair without turning themselves into accidental can-can dancers, that they could no longer walk arm-in-arm with a friend or partner, and could only greet someone by leaning forward and touching fingertips. It was social distancing before its time.

ღღღ

The crinoline was a product of Napoléon III's Second Empire. Since the slim lines of the first Napoléon's era, women's skirts had been getting progressively puffier thanks to increasing numbers of starched petticoats. In the early 1850s, up to seven layers were often worn, including a thick horsehair[56] underskirt to give extra bulk. According to some sources, this mass of fabric could weigh up to nine kilos. Presumably, in any weather except frost, it also heated ladies' legs to dangerously high temperatures.

Then, in the same way that the Second Empire was building railways and iron bridges, someone came up with a parrot-cage-like frame of steel, to be hung from a waistband. Once that had been invented, it was similar to the development of the skyscraper. With strong enough girders, the sky was the limit.

The Empress Eugénie's critics claimed that she personally conceived this impractical garment, but that is absurd – she was no engineer. What she did was see the crinoline's potential for excess, and begin wearing ever-larger models, forcing her fashion-addict female entourage to do the same. Soon women across the whole of France were imitating her.

A British crinoline frame in the Victoria & Albert

---

[56] In French, horsehair is 'crin', hence the name of the future crinoline.

Museum in London, dated '1860-65', was advertised when it was first sold as 'A Favourite of the Empress' – a clear reference to Eugénie whose power as an international role model cannot be overstated. That, of course, was why she was such a vital ally to the Worths, and why it was always so important to convince Eugénie to wear Charles's styles.

ღღღ

The invention of the crinoline is claimed by several countries, but the first patent was French, obtained in April 1856 by a company called RC Milliet. The manufacturer called it a 'skeleton petticoat' and boasted that it used the same flexible steel springs developed for watches. It consisted of ten hoops, narrow at the hips, widening out to its full circumference at the feet. The idea quickly spread, and an advertisement published in America in 1858 promised that the new cage crinoline combined 'lightness with extreme elasticity and strength [that] relieve the spine from the heat caused by wearing a great number of thicknesses, and thus obviate the evils of compressing the figure.'

The crinoline's manufacturers became even bolder with their boasts. In the 2 October 1858 issue of an American magazine called *Frank Leslie's Weekly*, there was a story about a woman who fell off a boat into a river and, despite the current, floated thanks to her light crinoline, so that she could be rescued. The same magazine later printed a story about a Canadian woman who was walking on a frozen lake when the ice gave way. Fortunately, she was kept aloft by her crinoline. It was, according to the advertisers, a literally life-saving garment.

These publicity campaigns worked, and the crinoline became so popular all over the world that the British satirical magazine *Punch* coined the mocking term 'crinolineomania'. One factory in London was producing 4,000 crinoline frames a day; another in New York used four tons of steel per month making crinolines, as well as 24,000 spools of cotton and 30,000 metres per month of whalebone.

The crinoline crossed social boundaries. As a mass-produced product, it quickly became affordable, and in middle-class homes, maids in crinolines were soon competing with their mistresses for floor space. The Worths were surprised to see their own concierge wearing one.

ღღღ

The crinoline naturally had its critics. The French writer Maxime Du Camp looked back on the era: 'Women were framed in iron, slim on top and enormous below, so that they looked like handbells. When one dined between two ladies, one was buried in their skirts.'

In May 1857, a woman called Jane Matilda wrote to *Punch* suggesting that the crinoline encouraged vanity in a woman by making her occupy 'more than ten times the space in the world than ever Nature intended for her.'

When women found that they could not sit on a conventional seat without showing off their thighs, designers came up with special crinoline-friendly chairs that left space between the back and the seat, giving the lady room to position the rear of her crinoline behind her as she sat down.

There were also frequent complaints from women who could not safely or decently negotiate staircases.

Queen Victoria seemed to agree with the malcontents. In 1858, when her eldest daughter (also called Victoria) married Prince Friedrich of Prussia, the Queen ordered the women of the groom's entourage not to wear crinolines to the wedding ceremony because the Chapel Royal at St. James Palace was too small to cope. This inspired a rumour that Queen Victoria hated crinolines, and *Punch* rewrote the national anthem in her honour, damning everything the crinoline stood for, including its Frenchness:

> Long live our gracious Queen
> Who won't wear crinoline
> Long live the Queen!
> May her example spread
> Broad skirts be narrowèd
> Long trains be shortenèd
> Long live the Queen!
>
> Oh storm of scorn arise
> Scatter French fooleries
> And make them pall.
> Confound these hoops and things
> Frustrate those horrid springs
> And india-rubber rings
> Deuce take them all!
>
> May dresses flaunting wide
> Fine figures cease to hide
> Let feet be seen.
> Girls to good taste return
> Paris flash modes unlearn
> No more catch fire and burn
> Thanks to the Queen!

The reference in the third verse to catching fire and burning was no joke. A woman standing too close to a naked flame could easily end up as a modern Joan of Arc.

According to some estimates, in Europe and the USA there were about 3,000 deaths between 1850 and 1860 caused by crinoline fires. Amongst the better-known victims were Frances Longfellow, wife of the poet Henry, who died in Cambridge, Massachusetts in July 1861, apparently while sealing an envelope with hot wax. In November 1871 Oscar Wilde's half-sisters Mary and Emily, aged only 22 and 24, were tragically killed at a dance in Ireland. One of them was waltzing past a fireplace which set her crinoline alight. The other sister tried to save her and burned to death in the attempt.

Of course, the main cause of these fires was the flammability of dress material, but the sheer width of crinolines was an obvious contributory factor.

Factory owners began ordering their female employees not to come to work in a crinoline. Not just because of the danger of fire: in 1864, an Irish girl called Ann Rollinson, a worker at a bleach factory, was killed when her crinoline got caught in a mangle.

ʊʊʊ

Jean-Philippe Worth's opinion was that his father was one of the crinoline's earliest supporters, and 'saw its possibilities at once and proceeded to introduce it.' Jean-Philippe claimed that this happened in about 1860, but he must be wrong about the date because in 1856 the Empress Eugénie was constantly in crinolines, and the fashion was already spreading down the French social scale.

However, it is certain that Charles Worth initially approved of the crinoline's lightness compared to the old petticoats that had formerly bulked out dresses. He was also intrigued because the crinoline allowed women to indulge in almost unlimited excess. As Jean-Philippe put it, at that time 'the ultimate in smartness was to have a crinoline so huge that one could not pass through a doorway.' This was reminiscent of Versailles in Marie-Antoinette's day, when hairpieces became monstrously high, forcing women to hold their heads out of carriage windows, and risk catching fire when waxed hair met low chandelier.

Charles also seemed to enjoy the way in which the crinoline created the image of woman as an unapproachable being – you literally could not get within an arm's length of her without stomping on her dress. And a woman could become a kind of disembodied doll, able to glide along almost magically because the movements of her legs and feet were invisible.

By 1866 or 1867, however, according to Jean-Philippe Worth, Charles had changed his mind and wanted to do away with the walking tent: 'My father came to the conclusion that the crinoline was becoming absurd.' Charles now thought that it 'deformed' and 'stiffened the female figure and robbed it of any charm.' He began his opposition with a half measure, designing a dress that was just as bulbous at the back, supported by a 'crinolette', but flat at the front from the waist downwards.

Charles's first dress in this style was made for a British client, and he was so pleased with it that he took one to show the Empress. Jean-Philippe Worth, presumably quoting his father, said that Eugénie's first reaction was 'an involuntary exclamation of delight.' But then 'she veiled her eyes at the very thought of being the first to wear a dress that was to her *impudique* (indecent) or at least "undressed" on account of its "flat" front.'

Eugénie assured Charles, 'That dress is perfect, I

couldn't imagine anything lovelier.' However, she added, she would not wear it herself just yet, and she suggested that he ask Pauline von Metternich to launch the new fashion. Pauline, the Worths' most faithful sponsor, duly took up the cause, created a social sensation wearing the flat-fronted style, and the Empress followed suit.

From then on, the crinoline was doomed, though it would take years for it to die out completely. And we should not forget that women were still destined to suffer suffocating bodices[57], wasp waistlines and huge bustles for decades to come. Charles Worth did nothing about those obligations – on the contrary, he embraced them wholeheartedly. But then he was no liberator of women. He was a clothes designer whose aims were purely aesthetic, and it was a coincidence that his influence on fashion contributed to reducing the danger of women meeting a fiery death inside their crinoline. His prime objective in life was to enhance female elegance – and, by doing so, achieve wealth, fame and prestige.

---

[57] It has been pointed out to me by Olivia Worth van Hoegaerden that tight-fitting bodices proved useful as back supports, and that, especially after several pregnancies, they preserved a woman's figure in an age before post-natal physiotherapy. On the other hand, of course, it is commonly said that Chanel 'liberated' women by ridding them of the tight Victorian waistband.

10 THE 'LITTLE HANDS' WHO MADE THE DRESSES

Charles Worth was the artist, Marie Worth the chief saleswoman, but who actually made the clothes? Who performed the minutely detailed cutting, sewing and ironing, often at top speed, that allowed Worth et Bobergh to maintain its reputation for high quality and swift delivery?

These workers were the *petites mains* ('little hands'), also known in French as the *cousettes* (a diminutive derived from the verb *coudre*, to sew), the *midinettes* (a word evoking women who go out to eat at midday) or the *grisettes* (a less flattering term inspired by the cheap grey material often worn by the working classes[58]).

If there were so many names for these humble seamstresses, it is because they were an omnipresent sight in the streets of Paris throughout most of the 19th century.

As their French feminine names suggest, they were almost exclusively women or girls – apprentice

---

[58] Ironically, in the same way that jeans evolved from goldminers' overalls into gold-diggers' fashion accessories, in 1927, Charles Worth's grandson Jean-Charles designed a chic grey winter cocktail dress called the *Grisette*.

seamstresses usually started in their early teens – and they were the highly skilled craftswomen who ensured that France became the centre of the fashion world. In 1851 there were an estimated one million French women working either full- or part-time in the clothing industry, out of a population of around 36 million.

ϖϖϖ

In Paris, most of these women lived outside the centre, in poor areas like Belleville and Montmartre. Those who were freelancers, paid a daily rate, often worked at home, but the luckier ones, with more stable employment, travelled every morning into the smarter neighbourhoods where the fashion houses had their workshops. During the day they were also to be seen out and about, delivering small parcels to clients and eating their lunch in parks or cheap cafés. Simply but stylishly dressed, with perhaps a touch of luxury in the shape of a hard-earned hat or a scarf given by an admirer, this daily tide of young women flowing along Paris's pavements naturally created its own mythology.

The French painter Jean Béraud, famous in the second half of the 19th century for his scenes of everyday Paris, depicted plenty of *midinettes*, usually attractively flustered while out walking, or anxiously awaiting a lover on a street corner. Théophile Steinlen, one of the Montmartre realists, also painted and drew them, though not always in such idealized poses.

The plot of Puccini's opera *La Bohème* centres on a poor Parisian seamstress called Mimi who is living in a garret in the same building as a struggling artist. She eventually dies of tuberculosis – the poor Parisian's traditional disease. The opera premiered in 1896 but was based on a semi-autobiographical novel published in

1851, *Scènes de la vie de bohème* by Henri Murger, who himself was a tailor's son, and presumably well acquainted with real *cousettes*.

ഝഝഝ

In 1895 a more light-hearted sociological study of the phenomenon was published by a writer and artist called Louis Morin. It was called *Les Cousettes: physiologie des couturières de Paris* (*The Cousettes, Physiology of Paris's Seamstresses*).

Morin describes the daily life of a typical *cousette*, toiling from nine in the morning until at least eight at night – even longer when urgent orders had to be completed – sewing thousands of tiny, tidy stitches that would be minutely inspected by the supervisor, the sales team and the designer before the clients even got a first glimpse of the garment.

And he writes that becoming one of these highly skilled but overworked *cousettes/midinettes* was no easy task. After at least three years of apprenticeship, which involved not only learning how to sew but also running errands for the qualified staff and putting up with their endless teasing, a girl finally became a seamstress, *une petite main* – if she hadn't been fired in the meantime. Only the best were kept on.

Amongst those who were talented enough to attain the status of a *petite main*, the least gifted might become a *manchière* (*manche* being a sleeve), generally a less complex part of a dress. If she wielded a more agile needle, she might be a *jupière*, concentrating on skirts (*jupes*) or a *corsagière* on bodices (*corsages*), or specialize in lacework or feathers.

Charles Worth is generally acknowledged to be the first *couturier* to divide his production line into specialized workshops, so that he had a whole department of *petites mains* for each different part of a dress.

Thanks to bosses like Charles Worth who were in the habit of accepting orders from important clients for next-day or even same-day delivery, the pace of work was fast and relentless. Morin captures this well: 'As the work is always late, backs hunch even lower, hands move even faster across the fabric, under the constant harassment of the supervisor who loses her temper.'

To make things harder for the girls, some workshop supervisors (older women who were often called *premières associées*) forbade talking, which gave Morin an excuse to depict the young girls as scatter-brained dreamers: 'When absolute silence is imposed, what do you expect the working girl to think about? This is when the latest newspaper scandal, read in haste that morning, becomes the subject of her daydreaming.'

If the girls were allowed to talk, often whispering 'as if in the confession box,' they discussed – *bien sûr* – love. According to the patronizing Morin, 'They chat about the morning's adventures, a gallant remark made by a passer-by, the cheap bouquet offered by a male friend.' Girls who are in a relationship talk non-stop about their paramour until their colleagues have had enough, and snap: 'You think he's faithful? While you're in here, he's got plenty of time to fool around!'

There was not only the hard work to put up with. The girls were also subject, Morin says, to the frustration of being poorly paid while 'folding expensive fabrics all day long, handling lace worth a hundred francs a metre and waiting for months to buy a miserable little twenty-franc dress.' Like diamond and gold miners, the women were working in a luxury industry without any real access to the luxury.

Outside the workplace, Morin informs his readers that the girls are prone to every temptation that comes their way. First, at lunchtime. A bell rings in the corridor and: 'There is a joyous crush, they all rush to put on their hat or fetch their little basket.' Some girls go home to eat, but others hurry to the nearest greasy spoon. Morin's mouth waters at the idealized spectacle of the *midinettes* erupting into the street:

> Midday is a pretty time in the centre of Paris. The young girls run along the pavements, released for an hour of freedom. It's the joy of a school outing, the happy relief of being able to stretch their legs, to laugh and breathe [...] They giggle at passers-by, and reply politely to a suggestive compliment with a happy quip. At this midday hour, the least graceful, the least refined girls look kind and appetizing, the pretty ones look adorable, and they prick a man's heart with the vague regret for something exquisite that he could perhaps possess, if he really wanted to ...

The girls cram into cheap restaurants and *traiteurs* (delicatessens) where 'the odour of ratatouille is mediocre but the portions are big.' These same places are frequented by young men, often poor students and artists, and the girls – usually in groups of two or three for protection – allow themselves to be chatted up. However, the chat ends with the meal: 'It is forbidden to accompany them out into the street. It's not the done thing. In broad daylight, it's unthinkable!'

Even so, after a quick lunch, once the girls set off for their half-hour digestive stroll, still in small protective groups, they love to be followed and exchange glances, or even words, with the men who flock around them. The girls fantasize (says Morin): 'We could, like the *cocottes* [call girls], make some money if we wanted to. But we don't want to!' Instead, they window shop at the jeweller's and start to think 'Why not want to?'

Predatorial men were forever buzzing around the girls. A comic postcard published at the end of the 19th century depicts an aged dandy with a top hat, cigar and a monocle ogling two naïve-looking girls. The verse on the card reads:

> Sans souci de tes cheveux blancs,
> Tu cours après les midinettes,
> L'Hiver fait peur au gai printemps,
> N'importune pas les fillettes

Loosely translated: 'Ignoring your white hair/You run after the midinettes/Winter scares joyous spring/So don't harass the young girls.'

The plea was usually in vain.

ღღღ

Like all poor women in Second Empire France, the *midinettes* had to find some way of breaking out of the poverty trap. The options for most of them were painfully simple: either marry a man with a steady job, become the long-term mistress of a well-off married man, or sell their favours. It was a calculation based on harsh economic realities.

Wages for the *petites mains* were generally low, and varied widely according to rank and speciality. In 1857, an average qualified seamstress was earning about two francs per day, compared to a male carpenter or stonemason who were on around 2.50. To put this into context, a kilo of bread cost about 40 cents, a kilo of beef one franc, eggs were 50 cents a dozen[59]. The women knew how to make their own clothes, and could buy a metre of cotton fabric or flannel for around one franc, or cheap taffeta for around 1.50.

But many girls in the workshops earned far less than two francs. An apprentice seamstress was unpaid, as the young Marie Vernet had been when training to be a sales assistant. In a report published in 1891 by Paris City Council, the most basic *couturière* earned only one franc per day; a *boutonnière* (buttonhole sewer) 1.75, a *plumassière* (feather worker) 2.50.

Rents in Paris varied hugely during Napoléon III's Second Empire, partly because old, cheap buildings were being demolished and replaced by chic *Haussmannien* apartments (see chapter 14 below for more details of these social changes). Most *Haussmannien* dwellings were relatively large, with at least a bedroom, living room and kitchen. The top-floor garrets, the *chambres de bonne* (literally, maid's bedrooms) were often occupied by the servants of the people on the grander floors below, so single rooms, highly sought after by poor workers like the *midinettes*, were relatively expensive.

According to a study published in 1872, in 1870, in rue Caumartin, near the garment district, an unfurnished top-floor garret (usually with no running water and a shared toilet in the courtyard) cost 220 francs per year. That is about 60 cents per day, for someone who might be earning only two francs – on the days that person was actually working. Days off were not paid.

---

[59] Despite attempts during the Revolution of 1789 to impose the metric system, the French still counted eggs in dozens. To this day, they sell them in boxes of six (or, less commonly, four).

Out in the poorer parts of the city, prices were barely lower because landlords overcharged to cover the risk that tenants might one day skip without paying, a common occurrence. In the east of Paris, in the rue Saint-Antoine (now in fashionable Bastille, but back then a deprived working neighbourhood) an unfurnished garret in a rundown building cost between 100 and 140 francs per year. Furnished rooms, with perhaps a bed, chair and a small table, cost at least double.

A worker on a daily wage, with no guarantee against unemployment, could never aspire to buying their flat. They couldn't save, and no one would lend them money. In any case, whole buildings usually belonged to the same owner who had bought property as an investment: rents yielded a return of anything between four and ten per cent per year, so owners hung on to their apartments.

All in all, Louis Morin calculated that a careful *petite main* might make about 35 cents profit per day, to put aside or spend on pleasures. So of course these young women dreamed of finding some other way of improving their lot. At fifteen, he says, most of them were virgins, but usually had an innocent '*petit amoureux*' (young admirer) who sent them romantic notes and stole a kiss at lunchtime. After fifteen, things got more sexual and more pragmatic.

Morin, the vicarious predator, actually reveals the formula for entrapping a *midinette* for sexual purposes.

There is no point trying to chat her up in the street, he says, if you are hoping for an immediate result: 'She will not surrender without at least the pretense of love.' The seducer, he advises, has to be persistent: 'If he follows her for a month, invites her out, pays for theatre tickets, for days out in the country, then it's different [...] He becomes the lover.'

As the ideal seduction venue, Morin suggests the île de Croissy, a long island in the River Seine west of Paris that was a common destination for weekend relaxation – it was easily accessible by train from Saint-Lazare, and there were café barges on the riverbanks. Claude Monet and Auguste Renoir painted famous pictures of revellers here, partying in their Sunday best.

For the prospective seducer, the thing to do, according to Morin, was to walk his *midinette* out amongst the willow trees, which, he says 'have seen so much open-air excitement that they seem to be accomplices in these idylls.' As the man ushers the girl along, he needs to become gradually bolder, first with an arm around the waist, followed by more ardent kisses, until she falls into a kind of trap woven by the willows: 'Their thick foliage, which comes down to ground level, envelops the lovers, hiding them from prying eyes; their roots, growing out of the sand, make walking difficult and prevent any chance of escape.' It doesn't matter if there are plenty of other couples doing the same thing: the 'unexplained laughter and suggestive feminine cries' all around only encourage the 'little worker' to give in.

On the other hand, perhaps as a warning to his male readers, Morin also depicts predatorial *midinettes* – more calculating, usually older, women who spot a well-to-do man in the street or in a Montmartre dance hall and ensnare him: 'Maybe he will make a husband; but certainly he will be at least a long-term lover.' Ideally the man and the *midinette* will live together; or perhaps he will set her up in a decent apartment and visit her regularly; at worst he will be generous with gifts. If she's really lucky, she may be able to give up work altogether. But Morin advises his readers against letting her do this:

> She will be bored, she will go out shopping, be tempted by the forbidden fruit of clothing, she will give in, overspend, run up debts [...] These pretty dresses will attract compliments, she will meet admirers here and there, and when her debts become too outrageous and her lover scolds her too harshly, she will enter the legion of Parisian women whose flirtatiousness leads them to cheat on their husband or lover.

Morin devotes a whole chapter to the horrors of disentangling oneself from a scorned seamstress. And he barely even alludes to the difficulties and dangers for a young woman of becoming an unmarried mother. With a detachment bordering on the inhumane, he concludes: 'Moral questions apart, what is the happiest ending for [the *midinette*]? Call girl, spinster or mother of a family? It is hard to say.'

Louis Morin, both creator and destroyer of the *midinette* myth.

ʊʊʊ

These, then, were the young women who made the Worths' social and financial ascension possible. Their destiny was typical of working-class women in Napoléon III's Paris, which was full of young provincials, male and female, who migrated to the capital in search of employment. The *midinettes* were just the most visible, and attractive, of the hordes of poor people desperate to make a decent living and improve their lot. And, but for a large dose of ambition, determination, talent and luck, Charles and Marie Worth might well have spent their whole lives in the same struggling social class.

Which is why it is satisfying to know that the Worths

recognized the true value of their workers. According to the Worth family today, Charles and Marie always paid their *petites mains* and the rest of their employees at least the standard rate of salary, or more, and offered chances of promotion to the most promising – those who most resembled themselves, perhaps. This is disputed by the biographer Diana de Marly, who alleges that the Worths and Bobergh did not concern themselves with their workers' welfare because they were 'too busy building up their business to stop and think about justice.' However, in its obituary to Charles in 1895, the French newspaper *Le Gaulois* noted that 'he gave all his employees a financial interest in his business,' paying 'excellent salaries.'

If true (and why would a late 19th-century French reporter miss a chance to snipe at a famous relic of the Second Empire?), this was not pure generosity – it made economic sense. With business expanding rapidly, Charles had to hold on to his most gifted seamstresses, and he needed them to rise up through the ranks quickly if they survived the pace of work and met the high standards that he and his clients demanded.

Moreover, we know that the most personable of the *petites mains* could be elevated out of Worth's workshops and into the fitting room, as *essayeuses* (fitters), overseeing the final touches to the garments. For this role, they had to look and act like refined young ladies – as Marie Worth herself had learned to do – while also adopting a Charles Worth-like persona as a creative genius. Louis Morin describes a typical *essayeuse* becoming as haughty as Charles Worth himself: she 'had to be almost a woman of the world, so that she would make a favourable impression upon the client, and almost an artist to be able to undress the lady with a single glance and judge how she could slim some shapeless lump down to an hourglass figure.'

Charles gave his most gifted *petites mains* excellent motivation to succeed. According to *Le Gaulois*, 'his top seamstresses and his saleswomen could earn from ten to twenty thousand francs per year' – that is a very impressive 30 to 60 francs per day. Jean-Philippe tells the story of a woman who started out as a *petite main* on three francs a day and worked her way up to being in charge of Eugénie's dresses, so that by the end of a twenty-year career, she had received so much pay, and had invested it so wisely thanks to the insider stock-market tips she received from high-society clients on developments like the Suez Canal, that she was able to marry off her daughter with a 300,000 franc dowry – an immense fortune, equivalent to about a million euros in modern France (so Jean-Philippe might have exaggerating *un petit peu*).

According to Jean-Philippe, Charles and Marie went beyond purely financial rewards. He says that they took a parental interest in all their *petites mains*, giving them maternity leave, helping out with accommodation and even setting up a company canteen – perhaps so that their *midinettes* would be less tempted by the distractions of the lunchtime Paris pavement show.[60]

In short, it seems to be true that the Worths were fully aware that these young women were key workers in the burgeoning fashion industry; the *cousettes/midinettes/petites mains* held Worth et Bobergh's success literally in their hands.

---

[60] Once the Worths' elder son Gaston joined the company, he set up the Mutuel des Couturières, a fund to provide sick pay and pensions to workers in the dressmaking business.

11 THINGS CAN ONLY GET BETTER

As the 1860s wore on, the Worths must have felt that their shooting star was never going to fall. Modernized Paris was attracting ever more tourists and rich foreign residents, and high-paying clients bombarded 7 rue de la Paix with orders.

By now, there were competitors for the title of Paris's greatest male dressmaker. Emile Pingat opened his fashion house in 1860, in the rue Louis le Grand, about 300 metres from the House of Worth. As of 1868, there was also the Maison Félix, near the Place de la Concorde in the rue Faubourg Saint Honoré. The designer there, 'Félix', was a 27-year-old from the Loire Valley called Émile Poussineau[61]. Working very much on the Worth model, both houses built up a reputation for stylishness, fine workmanship and high-quality materials.

Some female dressmakers were also breaking free of their traditional, passive role. Best known amongst these was Madeleine Laferrière, who designed for her father's company, Maison Laferrière, founded in 1869. Born in 1847, Madeleine was much younger and only started to become a serious rival later in the century.

However, none of these competitors could really

---

[61] The startlingly low-cut black dress in John Singer Sargent's famous portrait of *Madame X* is by Maison Félix.

match the selling power of Charles Worth's apparently inexhaustible creativity or the personal fame that he had achieved. Worth was the acknowledged leader of the pack.

ωωω

The Worths' client base now expanded far beyond the Parisian in-crowd. Aristocrats and royals from all over Europe were coming to Worth et Bobergh to be fitted.

The new continent of America was creating large numbers of millionaires who loved to sail over to Paris to spend a fortune on luxuries. Of course, at the time it was almost always the male of the family who paid the woman's dress bills.

Amongst the new captains of American industry was Isaac Singer, the sewing-machine magnate, who moved to Paris in 1860 to escape accusations of bigamy: back home, he had by then acknowledged 20 children by four mothers. In France, he quickly found himself a mistress, 19-year-old Isabella Eugénie Boyer (whom he later married and with whom he had six children). Isaac, a vastly wealthy man, was as generous with his money as with his offers of marriage, and sent Isabella to 7 rue de la Paix. He also did the same for some of his eleven legitimate and illegitimate daughters – though presumably not all at the same time.[62]

Another American fan of Charles's clothing was a lady mentioned earlier, the singer with the stage name Madame Moulton. She was born Lillie Greenough in Cambridge, Massachusetts, and at the age of fifteen was

---

[62] The Victoria & Albert Museum has a Worth dress worn by Clara Mathews, one of Isaac Singer's 'natural' daughters, at her wedding in London in February 1880. Singer was clearly a long-term customer.

taken to London by her mother to study singing. In Europe, Lillie met and married Charles Moulton, the son of an American banker, and moved to Paris where he was based. She was therefore that rare thing, a Parisian stage performer with a rich, respectable background.

By 1863, Lillie was spending much more time as a spectator than a singer, and was dressing in Worth outfits as proof of her place in high society. She befriended the Metternichs and then, while skating on the frozen lake in the Bois de Boulogne, she was introduced to Napoléon III and Eugénie. After that meeting, the American became a regular at events attended by the imperial clique.

Madame Moulton was a witty, sharp-eyed observer of social mores, and wrote countless letters home to her mother in which she gave vivid descriptions of her daily life. They were published in book form in 1912, under the title *In the Courts of Memory 1858-1875*, and make revealing reading. We see how the Worths had developed their business so well that their products were dominating the whole Parisian social scene.

Of one fancy-dress ball at the Tuileries in the 1860s, Madame Moulton writes: 'Worth alone made costumes to the tune of two hundred thousand dollars, and yet there were not four hundred ladies invited.'

The list of guests at this ball who were dressed by Charles reads like a *Who's Who* of the Second Empire:

Eugénie, according to Madame Moulton, 'was dressed as the wife of a doge of Venice in the 16th century [...] She was literally *cuirassée* [breast-plated] in diamonds and glittered like a sun goddess.'

Then there was Napoléon III's cousin Mathilde who 'looked superb as Holbein's Anne of Cleves' – an example of Worth taking inspiration from Tudor portraits, in this case a famous painting in the Louvre.

Not all the descriptions of Worth's gowns in Madame Moulton's letters are quite so gushing. She wrote that Augusta Bonaparte, the granddaughter of Napoléon I's brother Lucien, appeared at the same fancy-dress ball 'in a gorgeous costume of something or other; one had not time to find out exactly what she was intended to represent [...] but it did not look less brilliant for that.'

She delights in describing the revealing costume designed for Countess Castiglione, Napoléon III's notorious Italian ex-lover[63]. She was dressed as Salammbô, the Carthaginian priestess in the novel of the same name by Gustave Flaubert, published in 1862 (proof that Worth and his clients kept abreast of literary trends). La Castiglione's flimsy dress was 'without any sleeves, showing more than a usual area of bare arms and shoulders. The train was open to the waist, disclosing the countess's noble leg as far up as it went in black-silk tights.' For those prudish times, showing so much thigh was outrageous (and must have enraged Eugénie).

Pauline von Metternich, meanwhile, was 'dressed as Night in dark blue tulle covered in diamond stars. Her husband said to me, "Don't you think Pauline looks well in her nightgown?"'

Madame Moulton was sometimes outright unkind to the *grandes dames* of the imperial entourage, and for that matter to Charles Worth who was doing his best to glamorize them. She notes with a malign twist of the pen that he had dressed Anna Murat, Duchess de Mouchy, somewhat vulgarly, as 'a Dutch peasant with enormous gold ornaments over her ears.'

---

[63] Not so ex, according to rumours at the time.

Similarly, Countess Walewska, the wife of Napoléon I's illegitimate son Alexandre Walewski[64], who was Napoléon III's Foreign Minister, 'wore a Louis XV amazon costume, a most unbecoming yellow satin gown with masses of gold buttons sewed on in every direction.'

Madame Moulton was even crueller to Princess Clotilde, the 20-year-old wife of Napoléon III's cousin Napoléon-Jérôme, whose 'robe of silver brocade, standing out in great folds about her waist, was anything but becoming to her style of figure.'

As for Moulton (she leaves herself till last): 'My costume was that of a Spanish dancer. Worth told me that he had put his whole mind upon it; it did not feel much heavier for that: a banal yellow satin skirt, with black lace over it, the traditional red rose in my hair, red boots and a bolero embroidered in steel beads, and small steel balls dangling all over me. Some compliments were paid to me but unfortunately not enough to pay the bill; if compliments could only do that.'

This was just one *soirée* in a season packed with events, not only at the Tuileries but at the homes of various members of *la haute société*. It shows that Charles had now cornered the fancy-dress market too, and that Parisian parties had become Worth catwalk shows modelled by the cream of the *crème de la crème*.

Here is a list of costumes seen in early 1863 at two Parisian fancy-dress balls, as reported by *Le Monde Illustré*. Note the punchline at the end:

---

[64] Napoléon Bonaparte met Alexandre's mother, Marie Walewska, when he invaded Poland in 1807. She resisted his advances until her husband, a count, gave her permission to become the French Emperor's mistress, a position from where she might influence French decisions about the future of Poland.

Princess von Metternich's Ball:
Her Majesty the Empress as the goddess Juno.
Baroness de Rothschild as a bird of paradise.
Madame la comtesse d'Aoust as a bacchant priestess.
Madame C. Say as Madame de Maintenon [Louis XIV's mistress].

The Countess Walewska's Ball:
Madame la comtesse de Persigny as Fire.
Madame Rimsky-Korsakoff as Salammbô.
Comtesse Hahn-Hahn as an Incroyable [a male dandy during the Revolution].
Madame Brook-Greville as the goddess Bellona.
The very original costumes of these two recent balls were executed by Monsieur Worth.

Charles had moved from designing these prestigious ladies' gowns for everyday life into realizing their fantasies. He had become a type of guru moulding their self-esteem. He had turned them into Worth addicts.

Added to these Parisian get-togethers there were the week-long imperial house parties at Fontainebleau in the summer and Compiègne in the autumn, for which a woman needed at least 15 dresses – the maxim was 'two per day and one for accidents.' Pauline von Metternich once took 18 dresses to Compiègne, each one in a separate trunk.

Madame Moulton went even further: when she was invited to Compiègne for the first time in November 1866, she took 21 outfits, including seven ball gowns.

And Worth was the main supplier of all this finery.

In short, as the ball gowns, fancy-dress costumes and miscellaneous outfits for all occasions flowed out of 7 rue de la Paix, the money was cascading in.

ཀྵཀྵཀྵ

Throughout the 1860s, Charles Worth and Eugénie formed an ever-tightening bond of trust: she remained his most faithful – and highest-paying – costumer, while in return he was on permanent call to dash to the Tuileries whenever she needed him, night or day, and he kept her looking more glamorous than any other woman in Paris. As the *Sheffield Weekly Telegraph* put it when looking back over Worth's career in 1889, he made Eugénie 'the pink of fashion and the envy of all womankind.'

Eugénie bought her clothes and accessories from a host of different suppliers. Most of them were summoned to the palace at the start of each season, to receive a one-off bulk order. Charles Worth was the only *couturier* to receive spontaneous, last-minute commissions from her.

But contrary to the salacious rumours, the Empress always behaved formally towards Charles, maintaining her regal persona, though they were able to chat easily about social goings-on, the big issues of the day and, inevitably, fashion.

They had long discussions about fabric colours. Eugénie favoured strong shades. As Jean-Philippe Worth put it, she believed that: 'Lilac must be lilac, green must be green, blue must be blue.' Charles, on the other hand, had developed a taste for fabrics that teased the eye. According to Jean-Philippe, 'My father rather liked colours that were illusive and enticed the onlooker into wondering whether they might be mauve or mulberry.' Charles often had to back down and let the Empress choose her colour, while he decided on the outline, fabric and trimmings. Everyone in Paris knew that this was the creative partnership that kept Eugénie on her pedestal.

ʊʊʊ

Eugénie was also an active ambassador for Worth et Bobergh. Every time she received a state visit from abroad, any potential client in the entourage was introduced to the famous Englishman. Her guests included the wife of Franz Joseph of Austria, the Empress Elisabeth, popularly known as 'Sissi', one of the most famous royal beauties in Europe. In 1865 Sissi was immortalized by the German society painter Franz-Xaver Winterhalter in a full-length portrait (now in Schönbrunn Palace in Vienna). In it, she is wearing a spectacular off-the-shoulder gown in white tulle decorated with what look like golden flowers. The dress is commonly attributed to Worth. Despite a certain resemblance to a meringue, Sissi looks startlingly glamorous.

On 8 June 1867, with the creation of the dual Austro-Hungarian monarchy, Sissi was crowned Queen of Hungary. For the occasion Charles Worth created a daring off-the-shoulder dress with a bust-enhancing bodice inspired by a dirndl top. For decorum's sake, the new Queen's cleavage was covered up, but there is a photo of her, taken on that day, in which she looks decidedly provocative.

Another royal client sent to the rue de la Paix by Eugénie was Lovisa, Queen of Sweden and Norway. She was the wife of the confusingly named Karl XV & IV

(XV of Sweden and IV of Norway). He was a keen visitor to Paris and a devoted socialite who made sure that his wife always dressed the part whenever she accompanied him.

ღღღ

One of Eugénie's guests became probably Worth's most royal client ever. The Archduchess Charlotte of Austria was the daughter of King Léopold I of Belgium, a granddaughter of King Louis-Philippe of France, and a first cousin of Queen Victoria. The 'Austria' in her name came from her marriage to Maximilian, the brother of Emperor Franz Joseph I. She was therefore also the sister-in-law of Sissi, though the two were rivals rather than friends.

As a blue-blooded beauty of 24, Charlotte had spent her early life swanning around the capitals of Europe, but when she arrived in Paris in the early spring of 1864, marriage was about to take her across the Atlantic.

Three years earlier, in 1861, France, Spain and Britain had sent troops to Mexico to support a faction of royalists who wanted their country to be resolutely anti-American and pro-European.

Spain and Britain eventually withdrew their troops, but Napoléon III saw a royalist Mexico as a potential French satellite, so the campaign became a *cause célèbre* in France, and during the spring season of 1863, Mexican blue was the most fashionable colour in French high society. Napoléon III encouraged Maximilian to accept the title of Emperor of Mexico, as head of the pro-European puppet government.

Before leaving for Central America, Maximilian and his wife Charlotte were invited to Paris, where Napoléon III gave them formal promises that his troops would stay in Mexico long enough to establish their regime. To reassure them, the couple was ferried to an endless round of Parisian parties, balls and banquets[65].

Charlotte, who had visited her grandfather King Louis-Philippe at the Tuileries when it was a sober palace with few entertainments more exciting than embroidery, was dazzled by Napoléon and Eugénie's lifestyle – and not always in a positive way. She disapproved of the excessive opulence. When she was taken as a treat to 7 rue de la Paix for a fitting, she was apparently not Worth et Bobergh's most enthusiastic customer. Even so, thanks to Eugénie, this was a prestigious addition to the company's books, and Charlotte's week-long stay in town gave Charles time to fit her out with gowns worthy of a Parisian gala and, if all went to plan, a Mexican imperial palace.

ഗഗഗ

The pinnacle of the Eugénie-Worth partnership, and probably of the whole Second Empire, was the *Exposition Universelle* that took place in Paris between 1 April and 2 November 1867. It was an exercise in blatant self-aggrandisement by Napoléon III. Baron Haussmann's *'grands travaux'* were now more or less complete, and the Emperor wanted to show off his sparkling, airy new city.

Accordingly, an official Expo 1867 hymn was commissioned from Giaochino Rossini (it was one of his last compositions, he died the following year), entitled *The Hymn to Napoléon III and his Valiant People*.

A site was chosen – fifty hectares on the Champs de

---

[65] With dubious taste considering the Austrian couple's imminent fate, for one of the banquets the Tuileries' chef created a dessert called 'la bombe Mexicaine'.

Mars (where the Eiffel Tower would be built in 1889). Around 26,000 workers built a 200,000 square metre oval exhibition hall, in which American inventors Charles and Norton Otis were invited to demonstrate their early security elevators, and which contained an aquarium so huge that it inspired the Nautilus submarine in Jules Verne's novel *20,000 Leagues under the Sea*. Verne must also have seen the deep-sea diving suit presented by a New York company.

Ominously, one of the biggest spaces reserved on the (aptly-named in this case) Field of Mars was for the display of cannons by the Prussian manufacturer Krupp. Just three years later, these would be turned against France.

Wilhelm I of Prussia was one of the star guests on an impressive list of crowned heads invited by Napoléon III. Over the course of the *Exposition*, more than 80 members of royal families would come to Paris. These included Czar Alexander II of Russia, Ludwig II of Bavaria, Queen Marie of Portugal, Leopold II of Belgium, Sultan Abdülaziz of Turkey, and future monarchs such as Edward Prince of Wales and Prince Oscar of Sweden.

Most of the women in these royal entourages went to see the Worths. The team at 7 rue de la Paix clicked into overdrive. Charles and Marie took on extra staff, and their workforce now numbered around 1,200. Charles himself spent long hours at the Tuileries, creating dresses for Eugénie and then adding the finishing touches in her dressing room.

The main ceremonies planned for the esteemed guests were an opening gala, a parade and an imperial ball, but during the exhibition there were hundreds of grand events in the Tuileries and all the embassies, as well as Paris's noblest homes. For a few months, the city was to be the capital of the world.

The mood of the whole *Exposition* social season was playful. The Metternichs invited Napoléon and Eugénie to a party at the Austrian Embassy, at which a newly-installed door was opened to reveal a surprise guest in a specially-built ballroom: it was Johann Strauss, who had been brought in to conduct the first-ever performance outside Vienna of his latest waltz, *The Blue Danube*. Charles Worth naturally dressed Pauline for the occasion.

At public events, the ladies of the imperial court competed to see who could show the most cleavage. A prize-giving ceremony at the *Exposition* was transformed into a sexy fashion parade, with all the grand ladies appearing, as Jean-Philippe Worth describes it, wearing 'embroidered tulle dresses at two o'clock in the afternoon which glinted with diamonds and were cut as low as possible.'

Even amongst visiting dignitaries, relations were remarkably informal. A reception was held at the Château de Saint Cloud, where the renowned eccentric Ludwig of Bavaria was staying. Napoléon III went along, accompanied by all his ministers. He asked the Bavarian, 'May I be allowed to present these gentlemen to Your Majesty?', to which Ludwig replied, 'Certainly not. It would bore me to death.' Napoléon roared with laughter. Ludwig then conversed with Eugénie in Spanish, which turned out to be total gibberish. Eugénie let slip her regal façade and began to giggle.

Meanwhile in the streets of Paris, kings, queens and emperors could be seen strolling in parks, sitting unguarded in restaurants, enjoying shows, and admiring the displays at the *Exposition*.

Otto von Bismarck, the Minister President of Prussia, the man who in 1862 made the famous speech about political differences being settled ideally with 'iron and blood[66]', was seen at the opera laughing out loud at a new Offenbach musical called *La Grande Duchesse de Gerolstein*, a political satire that included a belligerent Bismarck-like character called Général Boum (in French, the onomatopoeia *'boum'* is, like the English 'boom', the noise of an explosion).

ϖϖϖ

Marie Worth was able to take in the sights and attend shows, but Charles barely had a second to spare. Before every official event at the Tuileries, he would go along to finalize Eugénie's outfit, more than ever taking on the role of an actress's dresser before a performance. On one occasion, when he had to prepare her for a ball, Eugénie was holding a bouquet of violets, and a few flowers fell to the floor. Charles leapt to pick them up for her, but then asked if he could keep them as a souvenir for a friend who was visiting Paris during the *Exposition*. Eugénie presented him with the whole bouquet. This, according to Jean-Philippe Worth, was one of the few times she was anything less than formal with Charles, despite their apparent intimacy.

It is not surprising that Eugénie was in a flower-giving mood. The 1867 *Exposition Universelle* was her hour of glory. All the unpleasant rumours about her past were long forgotten, all the criticisms of her over-spending seemed to have become irrelevant, and for the seven months of the festival she drove around Paris in an open

---

[66] Not, as many people think, 'blood and iron'. His original words were 'Eisen und Blut'.

carriage, usually accompanied by some head of state, being cheered and waved at by the crowds. She was now in her 40s but more glamorous than ever, and being maintained by Charles Worth and his apparently endless supply of stylish outfits for all times of day and night. Paris was in love with itself and its Empress.

Charles Worth himself was flying high. After the Metternichs' grand ball, he met Pauline and they discussed her social triumph. Charles told her, 'To think that it was I who invented you.' In her memoirs, Pauline said that she wasn't in the least taken aback by this claim from the man who, on the contrary, owed her his introduction to Eugénie. She simply commented, 'Perhaps that is quite true.' It seemed that Charles could do no wrong.

ϖϖϖ

Ominously, however, the extreme highs of the 1867 *Exposition Universelle* were counterbalanced by some lows that did not bode well for the future, either for France or for the Worths.

On June 6, Napoléon III held a military parade at Longchamp race course, near the Bois de Boulogne. Around 60,000 soldiers performed manoeuvres – an impressive-sounding number perhaps, but the army was very much a sideshow in Napoléon's France. He had promoted incompetent officers to be leaders (as one military historian[67] put it, 'his generals were well-meaning captains') and had not kept up with technological advances. Napoléon III's army was all about shiny uniforms and showy wargames. But his troops staged an

---

[67] Fernand Gambiez, in *Histoire, Economie et Société* magazine, 1988.

excellent spectacle, and on this sunny day the Parisian crowds thronged out to watch.

Charles Worth, busy at the rue de la Paix, was due to go to the Tuileries that evening to prepare Eugénie for a ball at the Russian Embassy. But a messenger arrived summoning him to see the Empress immediately. There, a lady-in-waiting explained that a rapid costume change was required, because there had been an assassination attempt at Longchamp.

Fortunately, the victim was not Napoléon III, the Worths' biggest creditor. The highest-ranking of the royal guests at the military review was Czar Alexander II of Russia. He had been leaving Longchamp in a carriage when a 20-year-old Polish emigré called Anton Berezowski fired a pistol at him. The would-be assassin missed: the gun exploded in his hand and he shot an equerry's horse in the head.

It was a doubly fortunate escape. Napoléon III had been sitting beside the Czar. It was also traumatic for Eugénie: she was travelling in the following carriage, along with Wilhelm of Prussia.

Berezowski was arrested, and explained that he wanted to liberate Poland from Russian colonization. His only regret (apart from the fact that his shot had missed) was that he had committed the offence in France, a country that sympathized with Poland's plight. Rather unsympathetically, France sent the young man to a penal colony on the Pacific island of New Caledonia, where he stayed until his death 49 years later in 1916.

The upshot of the assassination attempt was that the Czar wanted the ball to go ahead, but that Eugénie had decided that her dress was too festive-looking. She needed a new gown that was more subdued – while still making her look more glamorous than any other woman present, of course.

'Monsieur Worth, I know I can count on you,' she told him.

Charles had about three hours to perform a miracle.

Rifling through the imperial wardrobe, he found an evening dress that could be made into a ball gown with a few alterations. He sent word to the rue de la Paix, summoning a team of seamstresses with samples of cloth and his dressmaker's tools. Then he set about performing his magic, cutting excessive trimmings, adding rows of discreet stitching, simplifying the lines, and – taking no chances – wrapping the skirt in three layers of silver and white tulle, the official colours for an imperial ball.

He took the transformed ball gown to show Eugénie. It was now plainer yet strikingly original. The Empress's fitters made some final adjustments, she added a crown and a few jewels, and then emerged to get the approval of her chief arbiter of taste, Charles Worth. He was satisfied, both with himself and Eugénie, who thanked him profusely.

When Napoléon III came to see how the fitting had gone, he too was delighted, and congratulated Charles on reacting so quickly. But in reality, of course, the dressmaker had no choice – his reputation was on the line. Failing the imperial couple at this time of crisis would have been unforgiveable, and could have cost him his career.

ღღღ

Just a few days later, Eugénie repeated the request for a last-minute wardrobe change, again because of an assassination – a successful attempt this time. Political upheavals were starting to give a darker twist to Charles Worth's promise of rapid service.

For a ceremonial ball to take place on July 1, the Empress had commissioned what was, according to Jean-Philippe Worth, the most sumptuous gown his father ever made for her: 'The material, a magnificent dull *faille* [a material composed of flat, ribbed lengths of silk] of lemon colour with a pattern of Pompadour flower [i.e. rose] clusters, reminiscent of Spanish shawls, had been especially woven at Lyon. Alençon [lace with flower designs made in the town of the same name] – real of course – and bows of pastel lavender trimmed it.'

When Charles took the dress to the Palace, Eugénie 'gave a little rapturous cry at such loveliness.'

Sadly, though, the dress was never worn, this time because of events far away in Central America.

France's support for the fragile regime of Emperor Maximilian I of Mexico had not lasted long. Only two years after Maximilian's accession, in 1866 Napoléon III announced that he was withdrawing his troops under pressure from French public opinion. Charlotte, the above-mentioned guest of Eugénie and client of Charles Worth, sailed to France (on a ship called the *Impératrice Eugénie*) to plead her husband's case. Napoléon III at first claimed to be too ill to receive her, then sent Eugénie to Charlotte's hotel to dissuade her from causing a scene and giving him bad press. Finally a meeting of all three of them was arranged, but discussions became so heated that Eugénie pretended to faint. In the end, when Napoléon III would not back down, Charlotte suffered a mental breakdown and left France for Trieste, which was part of the Austrian Empire, her homeland. This was in August 1866.

In May 1867, the Mexican republicans overthrew

Maximilian, and the news of his imprisonment and subsequent execution by firing squad – on 19 June – cast a shadow over the festivities at Paris's *Exposition Universelle*. For the ball on July 1, Eugénie was advised to wear something less upbeat than lemon silk splashed with roses. Charles Worth was paid for his initial creation, and commissioned to provide something more mournful.

He dressed the Empress in formal white and silver tulle, embellished with diamonds – a traditional ballgown. Mathilde also attended, along with the other *grandes dames* of the court, many of them adorned by Worth.

The writer Gustave Flaubert was invited to the *soirée* and his account of that night[68] reads like a report for a fashion magazine. He noted, rather unsportingly, that Napoléon III's brown summer coat 'clashed horribly with his black trousers.' The ladies, on the other hand, looked wonderful: 'What a beautiful effect the women's long-trained dresses make as they walk around bare-chested.' (A bit of poetic licence. He must have been referring to their low *décolletés*.) The visions of female beauty inspired Flaubert to sidle into a corner for a smoke, where he mused on this 'scene set for passion. Oh to be eighteen and loved by a lordly lady[69]!'

The occasion was a great social success, but after the miraculous survival of Czar Alexander of Russia and the tragic demise of Maximilian of Mexico, the festive mood of the *Exposition* was tainted, and never really recovered.

---

[68] Unpublished during Flaubert's lifetime. Taken from the collection of texts in *Vie et travaux de R.P. Cruchard et autres inédits*, published in 2005.
[69] Here, Flaubert coined the word '*seigneuresse*', a sort of female lord of the manor.

Times were becoming unstable. Russian and Austro-Mexican Emperors had been attacked, and the writing was on the wall for France's ruler too.

12 A PALACE OF ONE'S OWN

During one of their frequent carriage drives in the countryside just outside the city, Charles and Marie Worth discovered the village of Suresnes on the banks of the Seine, just the other side of the Bois de Boulogne. A bridge had recently been built there, connecting this tiny rural outpost with the west of Paris. A lane led from the river up through vineyards to a wooded hilltop, the Mont Valérien.

On these slopes Parisians were beginning to build villas as weekend retreats, from where they could ride the short distance to join in the high-society processions around the Bois de Boulogne. It was peaceful and rustic yet convenient.

Today, there is still an oasis of vineyards in Suresnes, and the view from the hilltop takes in the Eiffel Tower, Sacré Coeur and – less attractively – the skyscrapers of the La Défense office district. In the 1860s the skyline was dominated by the domes of the Invalides and the Panthéon, the twin towers of Notre-Dame and the smoky rooftops of urban Paris.

That smoke, along with overwork, was affecting both Charles' and Marie's health. He was prone to headaches that forced him to spend hours or days in a darkened room. She had bad lungs: a bout of bronchitis in 1865 would effectively send Marie into early retirement. Charles sent her to the South of France to convalesce and excused her from her duties at the rue de la Paix. From then on, her main role in the business was showing off outfits at social occasions.

ϖϖϖ

According to Jean-Philippe Worth, ever since his parents' business had begun to boom, they had hoarded their cash. It was put through the books by their faithful cashier and then stayed in their safe, to finance the next season's wages and fabrics. By 1864, this safe was bulging with 'some four or five hundred thousand francs' in profit, Jean-Philippe says, and Charles declared that some of it could be spent: 'Now I shall be able to build something at Suresnes.'[70] The Worths bought a large plot of land – 15,000 square metres – on the slopes of Suresnes, about one kilometre from the Seine.

Their choice of architect for the new house was obvious – Marie's brother-in-law Denis Darcy, who had now become a specialist in church restoration. He also built railway stations (for the spa town of Vichy, for example), and designed the tomb of the painter Eugène Delacroix at the Père-Lachaise cemetery.

Darcy set about designing a villa, or rather a small château, in a style that could most politely be called Napoléon III, like the Opéra Garnier – that is, displaying every characteristic of 19th-century architecture except restraint.

---

[70] Jean-Philippe says that the house ended up costing 800,000 francs, the approximate equivalent at the time of buying a million baguettes. This was the price of the buildings alone, not counting the layout of the gardens and the flamboyant décor.

Beginning in 1864 or 1865 (various sources disagree), Darcy planned a building with (amongst others) gothic, Florentine, English and ecclesiastical influences.

Jean-Philippe Worth later described the house indulgently as 'original, that cannot be denied, but it was charming and delightful and distinctive.' (The gentleman doth protest too much, one thinks.)

To start with, Charles and Marie wanted a grandiose entrance porch to rival those on the palaces inhabited by nobles like the Metternichs. It was to be inscribed with the motto they had invented for the family: 'Obtenir et Tenir' (to obtain and keep), a remarkably frank reference to their rise from poverty to riches thanks to their hard work and business acumen. And, of course, the opposite of what Charles's father had done with his money.

The front gate was an iron portcullis topped with a moustachioed head – part Charles, part Viking – and decorated with twin sculptures of the animal he thought best symbolized him – the snail, which climbs slowly but surely to the top.[71] He liked to tell people that he had chosen it because 'I carry my house on my back and have no other possession than my talent.' Two more snails, in stone this time, were climbing to the apex of the entrance porch, towards a smiling sun. The porch, more a house than a gateway, is still standing today, and looks a little like the side entrance to a neo-gothic cathedral.

The house itself was a work in progress throughout Charles and Marie's lives. They added to it constantly until it came to resemble a small hamlet.

Initially, Darcy's design looked like a street of five different individual houses. A contemporary drawing

---

[71] His rise was so meteoric that maybe the grasshopper would have been more appropriate.

showing his concept from an aerial view, as if the artist were perched in a tree, depicted a driveway that curved through the gardens to a long linear construction.

Looking from left to right, this consisted of two large neo-gothic houses attached to a glasshouse conservatory, which connected with part of an 18th-century French château, and finally, at the other end of the row, another gothic-style villa. The two larger houses on the left had small annexes growing out of the walls that faced into the garden – a Renaissance porch and what resembles in the illustration the nave of a small church. All in all, the house was a giant, playful, 19th-century folly.

Charles and Marie asked for this original design to be altered, exchanging the two neo-gothic houses on the left for a construction that looked more like an inflated English Tudor cottage. Now the blend of different historical and geographical styles was complete. Well, almost: later, in the grounds, the Worths added a building that was a cross between a Mediterranean chapel and a provincial French railway station, equipped with bells and a clock (as mentioned earlier, churches and railway stations were Darcy's speciality). On top of the main house they also built a tall brick tower that was square, with a domed roof, rather like a French emperor's mausoleum.

ಠಠಠ

The imperial feel of the place did not escape the reporter from an English newspaper, the *Bradford Observer*, when he visited Suresnes: 'Near the railway station rises from within a high garden-wall a red-brick château, in the form of the letter L, with a towered and turreted roof. It is the residence of Worth, the Napoleon of couturiers.'

The grounds were conceived as a *'jardin anglais'*, that

is, more natural-looking than a formally laid-out French garden which typically had straight gravel paths bordered by razor-edged hedges.

In Darcy's drawing we see the area of garden nearest the house, with a pathway that twists across wide lawns, past circular flowerbeds, large trees and what looks like a lake.

Suresnes' Musée de l'histoire urbaine et sociale (Museum of Urban and Social History) possesses an undated watercolour of another part of the garden. In the foreground is a (slightly formal-looking) square lawn surrounded by shrubs. In the centre of the lawn is a sundial on a plinth. In the middle ground, a goddess (or is it a Roman emperor?) overlooks the scene. And in the distance, through a stand of mature trees, we get a clear view of the Mont Valérien. It is very eclectic, but it is a lush, attractive urban garden, clearly laid out by a professional, and would have employed several gardeners to keep it from overgrowing.

The Worths' only regret was that their land, comprising several plots, was divided in half by a public right of way, so they had to link the two sections of gardens with a bridge.[72]

Pauline von Metternich was impressed when she came to visit the Worths in Suresnes in the early 1870s. In her memoirs she recalled that: 'The garden was beautifully kept and contained an abundance of flowers and fruit. What struck me in particular were the thick groves of trees, among which lilies, roses, irises and

---

[72] In 1892 their son Gaston managed to annul the public right of way so that the family could wander freely from plot to plot. Coincidentally, Claude Monet's famous gardens at Giverny were also divided in two, but he never managed to unite them, and to this day they are bisected by a road.

cornflowers had been allowed to grow. It was the first time I had seen anything of the sort. The effect of these flowers seen through the green branches was quite charming.'

Pauline looked a lot less favourably on the house itself: 'As much taste as Worth had in relation to clothing, he lacked, in my opinion, for anything else. The villa in Suresnes that he enlarged, adding a wing here and a wing there, and pavilions and chalets, has the effect of a jumble of buildings that, being on an area that is too small for them, clash with each other.'

She was even less keen on Charles's later attempts to enhance nature. After the fall of the Second Empire, out of respect for Napoléon III and Eugénie, he salvaged some of the wreckage from their demolished palace. Pauline did not approve: 'From among the debris at the Tuileries he had acquired great blocks of stone and stray pieces of sculpture. With these he had erected a sort of ruin which stood in the midst of all these buildings. Placed as it was, the effect of this ruin was absolutely disastrous, for it overpowered and crushed everything that surrounded it.'

There is a photo of this 'ruin' in the museum at Suresnes. It looks as though a tall section of the outside wall of Rome's Coliseum – all archways and columns – has been erected on top of a rocky cave from which water is flowing into a tiny ornamental pond, where a swan is swimming and a marble lion is taking a drink. As Jean-Philippe said, it is 'distinctive'.

When it came to the interior décor, Pauline and other chic visitors to Suresnes could not help showing their condescension. The rooms combined Charles's love of beauty with a typically 19th century desire to fill every cubic millimetre of a home with a picture, ornament or heavy piece of furniture.

In her memoirs, Mathilde Bonaparte, a regular (though apparently not very grateful) visitor for tea, declared the interior simply 'ridiculous'. Pauline von Metternich was kinder, but not much:

> The rooms were magnificently furnished, but I must say I would far rather have lived in a whitewashed garret than in a certain drawing-room which was the pride of poor Worth's life. It was one mass of gold, satin, plush, embroideries, etc.; every chair was edged with gilt, and there were knick-knacks without end. Following Gambetta's[73] example, he had had an enormous silver bath fitted in his dressing-room, while a fountain of eau-de-Cologne played continuously in the adjoining room.

Marie and Charles were avid collectors of porcelain and glass, which were displayed all over the house in Suresnes. The diarist Edmond de Goncourt[74] ironized about this after coming to the house as part of Mathilde's entourage: 'Everywhere on the walls, [there are] plates

---

[73] A surprising revelation. Léon Gambetta is remembered as one of France's staunchest left-wing politicians. It was rumoured in 1879 that he had installed a silver bathtub in the Palais d'Orsay (on the site now occupied by the museum of the same name), his official residence as President of the *Chambre des Députés* (House of Commons). It seems that champagne socialism was not invented by Tony Blair.

[74] Incidentally, the Parisian diarist didn't know his suburbs very well. He wrote that the house was in Puteaux, the next town along the Seine.

from every era and every country. Madame Worth says there are 25,000, and everywhere, including the backs of chairs, there is crystal. It is a mayhem of bits of china and glass stoppers.' According to the Worth family today, by the time Marie died in 1898 there were 35,000 plates in the collection.

ಞಞಞ

After Marie's bout of bronchitis in 1865, she spent a lot of time in Suresnes playing hostess to her rich and famous visitors. There was, of course, a full complement of servants to run the house – cooks, maids, gardeners, valets, etc. Pauline von Metternich noted, with perhaps a whiff of irony, that: 'The footmen wore knee-breeches and silk stockings, just like the servants of any other great house.'

Unsurprisingly, the townspeople nicknamed the house '*le château Worth*'. In short, typical of Napoléon III's Second Empire, the Worths had become lords of their own manor, where they could invite princesses for tea and cake. They had become what Parisians people were now starting to react against – self-elected nobility.

In fact, even before they built their personal palace, the Worths' sudden social and financial ascendancy and Charles's influence on the Empress had already set jealous tongues wagging. Paris's plentiful supply of snobs, conservatives, frustrated socialites, envious businesspeople and discontented husbands were organizing the almost inevitable backlash against the two Anglo-French *arrivistes*.

13 SOME PEOPLE DON'T LIKE THE CUT OF WORTH'S CLOTH

Napoléon III's rise to imperial power had been even faster than his famous uncle's. In 1796 the 26-year-old general Napoléon Bonaparte was winning battles in Italy; in 1799 he mounted a coup d'état to become *Premier Consul*, and by 1804 he was crowning himself *Empereur des Français* in Notre-Dame cathedral. His nephew achieved the same rank in just under four years: on 20 December 1848 Louis-Napoléon Bonaparte was elected President of France, and on 2 December 1852 he declared himself Emperor Napoléon III.

In an attempt to legitimize their dizzy rise to power, both men created new aristocracies, ennobling supporters who did not owe their titles to previous monarchies. For the first Bonaparte, this was easier, because the Revolution had wiped out or exiled so many *aristos*. And he was one of eight siblings, as well as being surrounded by generals who gladly accepted the offer of a title. He simply elevated his entourage.

For Napoléon III, things were more complex. His court always bore a whiff of the *nouveau riche*. After the supposed wiping clean of the aristocratic slate in 1789, plenty of old-school noble families had returned to France when the monarchy had been restored in 1815, and they resented the upstart Bonapartes. By the 1850s, even some of the neo-*aristo* dynasties founded at the beginning of the 19th century by Napoléon I had had time to learn how to look down on people they considered their social inferiors, exactly like the snobs who lorded over France prior to 1789. As we saw earlier, the immediate family of Princesse Mathilde, a Bonaparte, did not think Louis-Napoléon a good marriage prospect before he became Napoléon III.

ϖϖϖ

As practising tradespeople, the Worths were not ennobled, but they benefited from the privileged status commonly accorded to artists in France. Once a painter, writer, musician or (especially in Napoléon III's Paris) architect achieved celebrity, they could hobnob freely in high society, just as actors, pop stars and sportspeople do today. However, even this meritocratic rise via the *culture française* route was not always smooth. The philosopher and satirist Voltaire had found this out to his cost in 1726, when he was beaten up outside a duke's house for making one joke too many at an aristocrat's expense.[75]

Charles Worth – a mere dressmaker, hardly an artist at all by traditional standards – was felt by some members of the Parisian in-crowd to be taking liberties far above his station.

The Worths never claimed to be the equals of the high-society people they frequented. To be truly accepted in Napoléon III's court, the commercial classes had to hide their origins with fancy carriages and displays

---

[75] For the full story of Voltaire's mugging, see my book *The French Revolution & What Went Wrong*.

of fabulous wealth, as if the *source* of their money did not count. The Worths, on the contrary, wore their commercial status with pride – after all, their appearances at social events were thinly-disguised marketing displays. More than anything else, they wanted everyone to know the name and address of their shop. Even so, Charles quickly forged a kind of friendship with Napoléon III, who was informal in private company. When Charles came to the Tuileries for a fitting with Eugénie, the Emperor enjoyed popping in for some male banter with the personable, unconventional Englishman, who must have reminded him fondly of his years of exile in London. Charles also had a plentiful supply of anecdotes about his customers, and the Emperor loved to gossip.

It was the same when Charles visited the nearby home of the Comte de Morny, Napoléon III's half-brother, whose wife was a faithful Worth client. Apart from Charles Worth, few ordinary men in Paris were on chatting terms with imperial blood.

Charles only ever went to the imperial palace on business, but Marie was invited to semi-formal events with the Empress, especially in the company of Pauline von Metternich, the most famous Paris socialite after Eugénie and Mathilde.

Marie also became a member of the elite set of women who would drive around the Bois de Boulogne, showing off their day outfits. This was a fashion started by Eugénie, after her husband had turned an area of waste ground in the west of Paris into an ornamental park of woods, flower beds and lakes during the 1850s, in an attempt to create Paris's own Hyde Park.

In the afternoons, the ladies of Paris's smart set would dress up and climb into their open carriages. Many of them would file down the rue de la Paix on their way to the Champs-Elysées. They would then trot along the avenue, turn left at the Arc de Triomphe and along the avenue de l'Impératrice (since re-named avenue Foch) and into the Bois de Boulogne. Once at the large lake, the carriages would drive the three-kilometre circumference at a slow enough pace to allow their passengers to admire – or criticize – each other's 'carriage dresses' and nod reverently towards the Empress and anyone else who was rich and/or noble enough to warrant a formal acknowledgement.

Another social game amongst the ladies who trot was spotting fake blondes. These were usually *cocottes* or *grandes horizontales*, Paris's notorious tribe of high-class call girls and part-time actresses who would shamelessly join the procession of carriages and flutter their eyelashes at the wives of their paying lovers.

Marie Worth was the proud owner of a *daumont*, an elegant open carriage drawn by four horses, and she would often join the parade, pulling out of her rue de la Paix courtyard into the fray. She would of course always be showing off one of her husband's latest creations, and would unfailingly attract almost as many stares as the Empress herself. So this too was marketing disguised as a social outing.

ʊʊʊ

The Worths also began to receive invitations to balls at high-society houses, to theatre and opera premières, and to private boxes at Longchamp, the racecourse opened in 1857 at the far end of the Bois de Boulogne. Again, they were often accompanying Pauline von Metternich.

And it was an opera première sponsored by Pauline that provoked the first outbreak of open hostility towards the Worths.

Pauline was always a controversial figure. Apart from her habit of appearing in startling new outfits, she smoked cigars and was not afraid to speak her mind in public.

She decided that the French needed to learn to appreciate the German composer Richard Wagner. Parisians, she thought, had become too frivolous in their artistic tastes. They loved Offenbach's comic operas but knew nothing about 'serious' music. So she convinced Napoléon III that Wagner should be invited to conduct a performance of his opera *Tannhäuser* at the Opéra le Peletier (the new Opéra Garnier was not yet finished). The Emperor agreed, and Wagner was duly commissioned to oversee his French première in March 1861.

However, the German composer was not attuned to Parisian musical customs. It was accepted practice there that every opera and operetta contained a ballet scene in the second act so that members of the Jockey Club, an elite band of rich gentlemen, could admire the dancing girls and select the one they wanted to sleep with. In mid-19th-century Paris, many dancers were forced by poverty into prostitution, and theatre dressing rooms were often the scene of sexual haggling. It was an accepted fact that Jockey Club members could swan into a theatre at about ten o'clock, after dining out, and be treated to a dessert trolley of dancers.

But Wagner refused to pollute his serious opera with a sort of harem scene. He was also highly critical of the standard of musicianship in the Opéra le Peletier's orchestra (whose players needed 164 rehearsals before Wagner was satisfied), and he was outraged when it was suggested that he might like to add some well-known singalong tunes to please the audience.

Journalists got wind of the discord at the opera house, and gleefully reported on every tiff and mishap. They knew that Pauline von Metternich was sponsoring the event, so it was easy for them to turn on this German-speaking ally of the composer. Suddenly, the whole affair became a nationalistic cause.

Knowing that the first night was going to be conflictual, Pauline wanted to look her best, and got Charles Worth to make a spectacular dress that she wore with her most garish and valuable jewellery. Second Empire Paris adored this kind of display, and she inspired gasps of admiration as opera glasses tracked her arrival in her private box.

However, the Jockey Club was not going to take her snub sitting down, so at one point, a few of them stood up and began chanting 'Le ballet, le ballet!' As audience members booed or cheered the interruption, Pauline smashed her fan on the parapet of her box, and shouted 'Imbéciles!'

Predictably, the partisan French newspapers rubbished *Tannhäuser* and mocked Pauline von Metternich's presumption that she could dictate Parisian taste. And because Charles Worth was known to be one of her favourite artistic causes, the journalistic knives were out for him, too.

ʊʊʊ

While a furious Wagner was packing his bags and leaving Paris in a huff, Charles and Marie had to deal with their first piece of overt public criticism.

Jean-Philippe Worth mentions a scandal-mongering article that appeared in a fashion magazine called *Le Follet: Courrier des salons*.

The journalist described an anonymous but newly-established fashion house that was 'being used as a peep-show by men about town.' Parisians would be able to guess which fashion house it was because the writer referred to its director as a 'man who received people with a "*calotte grecque*" [tassled cap] on his head and his feet on the chimney piece.' Charles Worth's taste for this type of headwear was well known.

The most hurtful aspect of it was that the journalist himself lived at 7 rue de la Paix, on the floor above the Worths. Perhaps the allegations of running a peep-show were wish fulfilment on his part – he was fantasizing about all the chic women he saw entering the building, and who no doubt ignored the poor scribe if they met him on the staircase.

Jean-Philippe defends his parents' morality: 'My mother, the shyest and most conservative of women, never was out of the shop, and my father's great reserve and sheer dignity – he never succumbed even to that mildest dissipation, a cigarette – were well known.' (At that time, Marie was often out of the shop showing off her husband's dresses, but a son's loyalty can easily tempt him to exaggerate.)

There was an even more credible argument against the idea that Charles's fitting rooms were hosting voyeurs who wanted to ogle half-dressed ladies: the Worths, who had just built up the most desirable client list in Europe, had far better things to do than run a peep-show. Their reputation was founded on classiness.

Even so, as Jean-Philippe put it, when the scurrilous article was published 'my poor mother was beside herself.' She rushed in tears to consult a client, Madame de Girardin, whose husband Émile was a well-known journalist. Charles had previously advised the Girardins on the décor of their home, and Marie knew that she could count on Madame's support. As Marie poured out her woes, Émile de Girardin was eavesdropping in the next room.[76] He stepped in and offered his advice: 'Dear child, don't worry. They are simply hoisting your husband to the top of the ladder. Don't say anything about it. Don't make any answer. Just let it go and see what happens.'

It turned out to be good advice. A few days later, the writer of the peep-show allegations approached Charles and offered to have the original article refuted and a flattering one published in its place. The price: 30,000 francs (a small fortune). Outraged, Charles refused to give in to blackmail.

In any case, the fashion house at 7 rue de la Paix had now become a target for ordinary Parisians, who flocked there just to stare up at the windows. Some of them were probably in it for a thrill, hoping to catch sight through the window of a semi-naked duchess. Others disapproved and would walk past with their noses in the air, as if the fashion house were a newly-installed brothel.

This happened fairly early in the Worths' career, but they must have realized already that it was the price of success: they had been thrown into the bubbling lava of celebrity and toxic envy.

ഗഗഗ

The key problem was that the changes in the fashion industry that Charles was instigating were just too shocking for many members of the general public – and more specifically, for men. Mid-19th century French males could not cope with the idea that Charles was

---

[76] Ironically, Marie's visit had turned into a kind of peep-show.

enjoying intimacy with their wives in the fitting room, even though many of the same men had mistresses themselves or visited prostitutes.

Here is another passage from Eugène Pelletan's book *La Nouvelle Babylone – lettres d'un provincial en tournée à Paris*, published in 1862 [77]:

> What is one to think of his [Worth's] client [...] virtuous perhaps, but forgetful enough of herself and her husband to spend an evening in a *tête à tête* with a male fashion designer debating about the depth of a cleavage, and to abandon to this worker of the vine the sovereign right to decide how well the leaf will hide the grapes. And they say that no Englishman will ever reign in France? But he reigns over the flower of France, at the foot of the Vendôme column[78].

It is obvious that the French male ego was feeling threatened by Charles Worth.

Pelletan went even further, and told the story of a *marquis* whose wife spends a fortune on clothing. When her husband stops funding her fashion addiction, she cuckolds him, and cries 'I am avenged!' Pelletan concludes:

---

[77] Dickens translated this section as well as those previously quoted, but he seems to have been so squeamish about the subject that he censored the more graphic Frenchman. So I have translated the passages here directly from Pelletan.

[78] The column erected by Napoléon I to celebrate his victory at the Battle of Austerlitz. It stands about 200 metres away from 7 rue de la Paix.

Would you believe that in this city of Paris, in this country France where the best-established fortunes are continually threatened by political tremors, there are mothers, there are matrons with so little foresight, and so little respect for the family's well-being, that they will parade around like prize cattle, wearing something like forty or fifty thousand francs' worth of frivolities, frittering away their daughters' dowries, or even their children's bread, on fashion designers' trimmings and frills? It seems that women are nothing but madly expensive curiosities that sensible men should do without.

The suggestion is clear: Worth, the creator and seller of outrageously expensive dresses, is threatening the very core of French society, *la famille*. Thanks to Worth, wives will commit adultery and children will starve. Men are even better off staying single.

ʊʊʊ

The novelist Émile Zola apparently agreed with Pelletan. He was quoted earlier, gently satirizing Charles Worth's adoption of an artistic persona, but overall Zola seems to have seen 7 rue de la Paix as a symbol of the unforgiveable decadence rampant in 1860s Paris.

La Curée was published in 1871, just after Napoléon III had been ousted, and in it the novelist looked back and painted a brutally satirical picture of the Worths' role in Second Empire society. It is a description that, today, often reads less flatteringly for Zola than for the victims of his irony. He is bristling with repressed sexuality and what the 21st century might call toxic masculinity.

It may sound unflattering to English ears that Worth is renamed Worms in the book. In Zola's time, the Worms were a French family of Jewish bankers and politicians, though given Zola's later defence of Alfred Dreyfus, it is difficult to believe that the name was chosen for anti-Semitic reasons. It was just a well-known name that started with 'Wor'.

As mentioned earlier, Zola is not purely negative towards Worth/Worms. He acknowledges the Englishman's skill as a designer. He also captures the sheer excitement a woman feels when wearing a Worth outfit.

On her way to an imperial ball, we see the heroine of the novel, Renée, 'trembling with nerves in the carriage taking her to the Tuileries. She was wearing a dress of prodigious elegance and originality that three of Worms' workers had come to her home to create before her very eyes.' Via the narrator, Renée seems to marvel at the ball gown's simple, daring elegance: 'It was very low-cut at the chest, in a straight line that was edged with a narrow band of lace, barely thicker than a finger. No flowers, no ribbons.' And later that night, when the Emperor spots Renée's lace-framed *décolleté*, the effect is instant. He murmurs, 'A flower waiting to be picked, a mysterious black-and-white carnation.' Mission accomplished for Renée. *Merci beaucoup,* Monsieur Worth.

But there is something about all this dressing-up that bothers Zola. One of the novel's protagonists, Maxime Rougon, is the son of a government minister who is making a killing out of Haussmann's redevelopment of Paris. After the death of Maxime's mother, his father has married a beautiful young woman, the aforementioned Renée, with whom Maxime begins a public affair. She is only one of his female conquests, but Maxime is portrayed as being very effeminate, apparently a symptom for Zola of the Second Empire's unmasculine frivolity. Zola describes Maxime accompanying Renée on a visit to Worth/Worms' premises:

> Maxime loved to live in the skirts, the rags, the face powder of women. There remained something girlish about him, with his long fingers and his beardless face.
>
> His favourite game was to accompany Renée *chez* the illustrious Worms, the brilliant tailor, before whom the queens of the Second Empire kneeled. The great man's reception room was vast, square, furnished with wide divans. [Maxime] entered with an almost religious awe.
>
> Ladies' outfits have a particular smell: silk, satin, velvet and lace blended their soft odours with those of hair and golden shoulders. The air of the room had this perfumed dampness, this incense of flesh and luxury which transformed it into a chapel devoted to some secret divinity.
>
> Often, Renée and Maxime had to spend hours in the antechamber, with twenty or so supplicants, awaiting their turn, dipping biscuits in glasses of Madeira, snacking off the large table in the middle that was laid out with bottles and plates of *petits fours*. These ladies felt at home, they spoke perfectly freely, and when they paraded around the room it looked as though a white flight of lesbians had landed on the divans of a Parisian lounge. Maxime, whom they liked

and tolerated because of his girlishness, was
the only man admitted into this inner circle.

Zola, typical of his time, clearly does not seem to understand why males – neither Maxime nor Worth alias Worms – should associate themselves with such an inherently 'female' activity, why they should 'live in the skirts of women'. Symbolically it is as if Zola were accusing them of being transvestites.

It was, of course, an extension of this attitude that would see Oscar Wilde imprisoned 25 years later.

ꟽꟽꟽ

As we saw in the Prologue, the crossing of sexual boundaries upset the encyclopedist Pierre Larousse so much that he turned a long section in volume five of his supposedly factual *Grand dictionnaire universel du XIXe siècle* (*Large Universal Dictionary of the 19th Century*) into a personal attack on male dressmakers.

It is worthwhile to look at Larousse's entry for '*couturier*' in more detail.

It begins with an historical note to the effect that in 1675, Louis XIV published a royal edict saying that only women should make women's clothing: it was 'becoming and appropriate to the decency and modesty of women and girls to allow them to be dressed by persons of their own sex.' Even so, Larousse informs us, women could only sew the clothing that actually touched the women's skin, because under this new edict, men – tailors – kept the right to make the dresses that covered undergarments. To ensure that women could not become fully fledged dressmakers, there was even a law forbidding females from keeping large amounts of fabric in their home. It was only after the Revolution of 1789 that this outmoded rule was scrapped. *Liberté* and *égalité* at last.

After this history lesson, Pierre Larousse concludes:

> Now that professions are liberalized, it would seem natural that women should have their adjustments done by women. But here, in the Second Empire, we are seeing the indescribable peculiarity of men (are they really men?) presiding over the outfitting of women from the uppermost classes of society – crumpling gauze over the breasts of princesses, placing ribbons and flowers on the bodices of duchesses [...] This is a fashion which, we hope, will not become a custom, and will not spread to simple, honest women. Let us leave to female hands the privilege of creating the outfits for our mothers, our wives and our sisters; let us leave them in the delicate care of an industry that, we know, requires a fairy's fingers, not the build of an athlete, if it is to be done appropriately and, above all, decently.

As if to demolish his own defence of women dressmakers against the patriarchy, Larousse ends with a sexist rant about women spending too much on clothes:

> We all know how big the dressmaking chapter in the household accounts book can be. Let us not dwell on it, for fear of re-opening cruel wounds in the heart of more than one husband [...] Flicking through the *Gazette des Tribunaux* [the journal of court records] we can see what it costs certain

fashionable and decadent[79] women to be beautiful for one evening – or to *look* it, anyway. A princess, sued for the payment of her dress bills, offered the malign eye of the public a glimpse into the morality of a certain social class.

Pierre Larousse seems to be confusing the issue. He is in favour of women *making* women's clothes, but he does not want women to *buy* them. More exactly, he does not want wives to spend too much on clothes, for fear of upsetting their husbands. He is also warning lower-class women against behaving like upper-class ladies. In fact, like Eugène Pelletan, he seems to be issuing an all-encompassing patriarchal alert to French females: Charles Worth and his ilk are dangerously amoral, potential homewreckers. It is best, Mesdames, to be content with your old clothes.

And all this, remember, was in a *dictionary*.

ʊʊʊ

It is true that the excessive cost of *haute couture* was causing problems in society and provoking gossip in the press. In May 1870, *Le Figaro* reported on a dispute between a countess and her dressmaker, Madame Achard, over what the client alleged to be an excessive bill. The issue was, the countess's lawyer said, that 'Madame Achard is not an ordinary dressmaker[80]. She does not belong to that old school of suppliers whose prices were fair and whose profits were honest. She is

---

[79] In French, Larousse refers to the '*demi-monde*', the decadent but public world of Parisian adulterers and courtesans.
[80] The French word used is '*modiste*', a simple maker of fashion.

from the new school, and you know it well, the immortal Worth is its leader. In other words, Madame Achard is not a maker, she is an artist. [Her] dresses are not dresses. They are creations.' The lawyer's irony is reported gleefully by *Le Figaro*'s writer.

The rant ends with a more direct attack: 'This cheap lyricism [on the part of Madame Achard] is perfectly ridiculous, I know, and these days it only fools a few old English ladies who are besotted by French fashion. Nevertheless, the seller, thanks to the overblown compliments she pays herself, ends up believing she is a genius and charges more for a dress than a fashionable painter would for a painting.'

In her defence, Madame Achard produced a letter from a satisfied customer, the vicomtesse de Fleury, saying that 'the Emperor looked at me and declared me charmingly dressed.'

In the end, the judge adjourned the case, declaring himself incapable of assessing the true value of a woman's gown. He even made a joke about not knowing the price of his own robes – a French pun, as '*robe*' also means dress.

But the important thing about *Le Figaro*'s article, and the trial itself, seems to be not the verdict but the tone. The reporter even transcribes the defence lawyer's words as he goes on to ironize about the way his sovereign, Napoléon III, is capable of causing inflation in clothes prices, adding: 'This is yet another responsibility that the Emperor is not concerned about.' In 1870, it is almost as if the whole Second Empire is on trial for overspending.

In *La Curée*, Zola uses Worth/Worms' exorbitant bills as a core mechanism of his plot. First, Renée's husband complains that she owes the Englishman 36,000 francs. When it rises to 50,000, Renée considers selling a jewel that she recently received as a present to pay off her debt. She makes several part payments, but keeps ordering extravagant dresses so that she soon owes Worth/Worms 200,000 and is worried about 'the scandal of a court case, and especially about falling out with the illustrious dressmaker.' The cost of these outfits even provides Zola with the closing lines of his novel: 'When Renée died the next winter of acute meningitis, it was her father who paid her debts. Worms' bill amounted to two hundred and fifty-seven thousand francs.' It is as though Renée is the ultimate fashion victim, cause of death: an overdose of Worth gowns.

ΩΩΩ

Well before these attacks by Larousse, *Le Figaro* and Zola, the Worths must have been aware that a section of the French middle-class establishment was accusing them of behaving little better than drug dealers or loan sharks.

As their profits boomed thanks to the opportunistic climate created by the Second Empire, Charles and Marie probably sensed that they were taking part in a risky game that wasn't entirely moral. They were charging truly exorbitant prices.

But then again, they were taking this money from the ultra-rich, many of whom could genuinely afford such luxury. And this was an age without a social safety blanket. There was no subsidized health service, there were no pensions (except those granted as rewards by kings and emperors), so people had to harvest good fortune while the sun shone.

The Worths knew this from personal experience. They both came from families who had seen hardship. Charles's father had lost everything, reducing him to little more than a printer's slave. He had fought his way out of poverty and had no intention of going back.

༒༒༒

Zola depicts this precarious economic climate in another of his novels, *Nana*. Published in 1879, its plot opens in 1867, at the height (or in Zola's view, low point) of the Second Empire.

The girl in the title is a fairly typical product of the *demi-monde*. To escape from her desperately poor background, the teenaged Nana, who already has an illegitimate baby, becomes an actress despite her complete lack of talent. She has one thing to sell: herself.

After every performance, her dressing-room is jammed with male admirers. She usually appraises them all and then agrees to sleep with the richest man in the pack. She 'entertains' so often that her dream is to spend one night alone in her own bed. She becomes a celebrity, and at a Longchamp race meeting attended by the imperial entourage, a filly called Nana (after her) wins a race and the crowd chants her name.

But the cost of her luxurious life begins to bankrupt her lovers one after the other, and she eventually has to skip town. In a brutally symbolic ending, she dies disfigured by smallpox.

Nana was meant to represent the Second Empire's moral decline, but the modern reader will sympathize with her. Poor and uneducated, she has only one way out, and a short-lived one: her youthful femininity. The luckier or more rapacious of the real Nanas in Paris exploited their rich suitors to the full, and then cashed in. The operetta singer and serial mistress Hortense Schneider, one of Zola's real-life inspirations for *Nana*, built herself a house in the west of Paris and, once she had saved enough, withdrew from society to live there with her disabled son. It was a hard-earned retirement.

ꙮꙮꙮ

Nevertheless, in the eyes of some envious Parisians, people like the Worths, who frequented and made money from the imperial entourage, and who dressed both the *aristos* and the Nanas, were tainted by association.

In the late 1860s they began to notice signs that the days of unlimited profits might be coming to an end. Perhaps in an attempt to gain popularity, Napoléon III freed the press from censorship, which meant that criticisms of the regime and its excesses appeared with increasing frequency in the newspapers (as we saw above with *Le Figaro*). Even when their name wasn't mentioned, the Worths shuddered to read the attacks on the high society they outfitted. One day, Pauline von Metternich told them that her carriage had been insulted as she drove along the rue de Rivoli. It must have felt like 1789 was coming around again.

Nevertheless, throughout 1868 and 1869, orders for dresses still flowed into 7 rue de la Paix. The mood at imperial balls was as carefree as ever. And in the autumn of 1869, when Eugénie and her ladies-in-waiting went to Egypt to open the Suez Canal, they were accompanied by literally trunkloads of Worth creations – about 60 or 70 outfits per lady, some 250 dresses in all.

This was probably the biggest and most prestigious commission that Worth et Bobergh ever received, but it was also the swan song of the Second Empire. As the Suez Canal opened, the orders from the Palais des Tuileries were about to dry up.

14 THE END OF AN ERA

At the end of the 1860s, few of Napoléon III's subjects would have contested that their country had made great leaps forward. At last, they had begun to compete in the Industrial Revolution that had been delayed in France by political unrest throughout the first half of the 19th century. The website *Napoleon.org* goes so far as to state that 'modern France was born under Napoléon III.' But then it is a Bonapartist website.

The achievements were impressive: in terms of pure national wealth, between 1848 and 1870 the Banque de France's stock of gold increased eightfold. A modern banking system was set up, enabling public and private institutions to take out loans to finance their development projects (and Napoléon III's regime took full advantage of this). For smaller savers, the first cheques became available.

The number of kilometres of French railway increased more than sixfold, from 3,600 in 1850 to 23,300 in 1870, almost catching up with the train-mad Brits[81]. In 20 years, the amount of cargo carried across France by rail was multiplied by ten. At the same time,

---

[81] In 1850 Britain already had 10,000 kilometres of rail; in 1870, 25,600.

the ports of Le Havre, Nantes, Bordeaux and Marseille were expanded to facilitate burgeoning international trade, and the networks of roads and canals were substantially increased. On top of all this, it was money raised at the Paris stock exchange that financed the world's greatest engineering project to date, the Suez Canal.

ཀྑཀྑཀྑ

We have already mentioned Baron Haussmann's new boulevards, but he did much more than create tree-lined avenues. Practically every straight, wide street in Paris today is the result of Napoléon III's desire to give France a modern capital city. Vast numbers of what we now consider typically Parisian six-storey apartment buildings with their zinc rooftops, fifth-floor balconies and roomy entrance halls date back to the Second Empire. It is estimated that, thanks to Haussmann's clearances, 20,000 houses were demolished and 43,000 apartment buildings erected.

The same period saw the construction of iconic locations like the glass market pavilions of Les Halles, the Place de l'Étoile around the Arc de Triomphe, the Jeu de Paume and Orangerie exhibition spaces, the huge Halle de la Villette abattoirs, the Place Saint-Michel, the Place du Louvre and many of Paris's twenty Hôtels de Ville (*arrondissement* town halls). Not to mention the over-encrusted jewel in the crown of Second Empire architecture, the aforementioned Opéra Garnier. Thanks to Hausmann, about 60% of the city's surface area was renovated.

However, below the surface, this modernized Paris was less clean than it looked: many of these building schemes enabled men[82] in the Emperor's entourage to earn more-than-healthy profits.

There were several straightforward, if semi-legal, ways to do this. The expropriation and demolition of buildings was financed by the state, and it was widely alleged that insiders received prior warning of which buildings were to be demolished, and bought them up cheaply before demanding an inflated price for their compulsory purchase.

These same investors could then benefit from the urban renewal by buying back the cleared land from the city and building large, chic apartments that would fetch high rents. Whole neighbourhoods were transformed from low-rise, run-down slums to six-storey bourgeois havens, with private developers making money at every stage. It was a classic case of the rich getting richer while the poor got nothing.

Much of the criticism for this was aimed at Haussmann himself, and by extension to his master, Napoléon III.

In 1870, the anti-Bonaparte politician Jules Ferry, who would be prime minister and introduce free primary schools for boys and girls once France became a republic again, published a pamphlet called *Les Comptes fantastiques de Haussmann* (*Haussmann's Fantasy Accounts*[83]) in which he defended the 'population whom [Haussmann] has been controlling, taxing, indebting, squeezing for the past fifteen years.' Ferry lamented the demise of medieval Paris 'where the craftsman, who is now being

---

[82] A reminder: in 19th century France it was very difficult for women to make a profit in business, or even to own a business.
[83] The French title is a pun on *Les Contes fantastiques d'Hoffman*, the collected fairytales by the German Romantic writer E.T.A. Hoffmann.

systematically and pitilessly chased out of the centre, lived side-by-side with the financier, where intelligence was prized more than wealth.' Ferry went further, accusing Napoléon III's regime of 'destroying the entire future on a bonfire of their whims and vain glory.'

Jules Ferry was idealizing the old Paris in which cholera, tuberculosis and typhoid were constant threats, but it was true that the working classes were now priced out of living in the centre of Paris, except as servants in the tiny top-floor *chambres de bonne*.

The population of the old medieval centre of Paris, the first *arrondissement*, fell from 89,000 in 1861 to 74,000 in 1872. Meanwhile, on the outskirts of the city, in unrenovated areas still polluted by factory smoke and often lacking basic sewage and clean water, population densities rose dramatically: for example, in the 20th *arrondissement*, from 70,000 residents in 1861 to almost 93,000 in 1872. In all, about a quarter of all Parisians were forced to move home by Haussmann. Rebellious rumblings were inevitable.

ʊʊʊ

No doubt because of the constant threat of a new revolution, the wide avenues did much more than provide space for opera-goers' carriages to get to the theatre on time: Napoléon III's contemporaries alleged that the boulevards were designed to be harder to barricade than the narrow streets they replaced, and wide enough to allow an army to march into the city and quell a revolt. In short, Haussmann was imposing Napoléon III's authoritarianism on the famously fractious city.

The Emperor was right to be afraid. He was in favour, in theory at least, of social reform, but he was first and foremost a capitalist, and left the question of decent wages and working conditions to employers, who predictably proved less than generous. And the French working classes are famous for objecting violently to social injustice.

There were so many attempts to depose or kill the Emperor that in 1870, just before the fall of his regime, a book was published, *Attentats et complots contre Napoléon III, histoire complète des attentats et des complots jusqu'à ce jour, accompagnée de portraits et de gravures* (*Assassination attempts and plots against Napoléon III, a complete history of the attacks and plots until now, accompanied by portraits and illustrations*). Note that 'until now'.

Some of these assassination attempts were committed by foreign agents who objected to France's foreign policy, but there were plenty of homegrown rebels. The book describes a full-blown revolution against '*la terreur bonapartiste*' that was planned as soon as Napoléon III declared himself Emperor in 1852. Then in June 1853 a shooting was plotted in Paris by 'three individuals of the working class'. The police got wind of it and arrested the plotters. The following year, half a dozen Frenchmen planned to plant a bomb on the railway line between Lille and Calais to blow up the imperial train. And in 1855 two shots were fired at Napoléon and Eugénie by a 22-year-old man from Rouen 'of vulgar appearance.'

ʊʊʊ

As his regime went on, the Emperor's non-Parisian enemies were increasingly enraged because the rest of France lost out during the beautification of the capital – a resentment that exists to this day. By 1870, Paris was the most indebted city in Europe, and the French banks that loaned the money had yawning holes in their accounts. Development in provincial France ground to a halt. In fact, the French state only managed to pay off the Paris-related debts to its banks after the First World War, when the franc had fallen so low in value that the reimbursement cost a relatively small amount of the nation's gold reserves.

Rumours of massive state debts and private profiteering were made all the more damaging because, as we have already seen, Napoléon III behaved as regally as any of France's deposed or beheaded monarchs. As well as organizing the flamboyant social functions that made the Worths' fortune, the Emperor appropriated some of France's most splendid châteaux for his own use: he occupied and redecorated the Palais des Tuileries in the centre of Paris, the Château de Saint-Cloud just to the west of the city, where he often housed visiting heads of state, the 1,500-room Château de Fontainebleau, the 1,300-room Château de Compiegne, and the ruins of the spectacular medieval castle at Pierrefonds, northeast of Paris, where his renovations were so expensive and ambitious that they were never finished.

Pierrefonds is an interesting case study in Second Empire excess. The ruins of the castle were officially declared a *'monument historique'* in 1848, but as of 1857 Napoléon III decided to transform it into a combination of private holiday home and showroom for the country's technology and craftsmanship. He commissioned France's best-known architect, Eugène Viollet-le-Duc, to draw up renovation plans, and then engaged top engineers, stonemasons, woodworkers, decorators and furniture designers to create a sort of Disneyland-style version of a medieval castle, conveniently next to a mineral water spa that would work wonders for the overtaxed imperial digestive system. It was literally a folly, and Napoléon III's regime collapsed before the work was even half-finished. Today the château is a beautiful but empty tourist attraction.

ღღღ

Louis Philippe, the king ousted by Napoléon III's coup d'état, had tried to avoid being tarred with the same brush as his royal predecessors by portraying himself as a bourgeois citizen, dressing drably in public except during official ceremonies. For the same reason, he democratized his title, calling himself 'King of the French' instead of the 'King of France'[84], and introduced a British-style constitutional monarchy. But it did not save him, because when push came to shove, he showed typical royal callousness towards his people. He allowed his army to kill 600 workers demonstrating over reduced wages in Lyon, and sent 40,000 troops to tear down barricades in the centre of Paris, where they killed all the residents of a building from which they had been fired on. He wasn't exactly an ordinary bourgeois Frenchman.

Napoléon III and Eugénie seem to have learned nothing from recent French history. As early as 1854, just six years after the fall of the monarchy for the fourth time since 1789, Eugénie posed as Marie-Antoinette for a full-length portrait by society painter Franz Xaver Winterhalter. Wearing a golden crinoline dress, she stands in a flowery bower, almost facing away from the viewer as if she is gazing dreamily into an idyllic past when French queens could spend half the country's budget on ear-rings. In the last few years of Eugénie's

---

[84] Admlittedly, to modern ears it does not sound like a great democratic shift.

reign, critics took to calling her '*L'Espagnole*' (the Spanish woman), a direct reference to the way that Marie-Antionette had been dismissively dubbed '*L'Autrichienne*' (the Austrian woman).

ʊʊʊ

Despite growing dissatisfaction with Napoléon III and Eugénie's public image, it was not their lifestyle that sank the imperial couple.

As the regime creaked on, its political opponents grew more vocal and more confident. In the parliamentary elections of 1869 (Napoléon III was not a total despot, and ruled via parliament), his supporters gained 4.6 million votes, but republicans took 3.3 million, most of them concentrated in the cities and larger towns. In January 1870 the Emperor felt obliged to calm tensions by naming a prime minister from the opposition camp, at the head of a compromise cabinet of ministers drawn from different parties across the political spectrum.

Then war raised its head. In July 1870, France and Germany disagreed over the succession to the Spanish throne (the idea of placing a Bonaparte there was of course one of Napoléon III's reasons for marrying Eugénie). The Spanish offered the throne to a Prussian prince, Leopold of Hohenzollern, on the grounds that he was a cousin of the powerful Kaiser Wilhelm I of Prussia and, even better, that he was not French.

After French complaints about this, on July 12 Leopold refused the offer to rule Spain, but Otto von Bismarck, the Kaiser's president, saw the disagreement as a chance to provoke war with France and thereby grab Alsace and Lorraine, the eternally disputed territories on the Rhine. In a decidedly modern move, Bismarck published a telegram in the international press, distorting a polite communication from the Kaiser declining a meeting, and making it sound like a diplomatic incident: 'The Kaiser refused to receive the French ambassador and informed him via an assistant that His Majesty had nothing more to say.'

As Bismarck had planned, this perceived snub provoked excitable anti-Prussian articles in French newspapers and on July 14 (Bastille Day) Haussmann's new boulevards were crammed with belligerent Parisians shouting 'to the Rhine!'. They wanted war.

Napoléon III, seeking to bolster his reputation and his regime, fell into Bismarck's trap and declared war on July 19, even though his own army was only half the size of Prussia's. Despite his ill health (aged 62, Napoléon was suffering from severe rheumatism, piles, bladder stones, and he had had a heart attack in 1864), the Emperor rode out to the German border, and on September 2 personally led his army into a massive Prussian ambush at Sedan, some ten kilometres inside the French border. Ironically, when Napoléon declared his intention to retreat back to safety in Paris, Eugénie sent a message urging him to fight on. It was an extreme example of: 'Don't come home until you've got the job done.'

After failing to die a martyr's death in battle, the hopelessly surrounded Emperor of France surrendered to the Kaiser and was sent into internment at a rather pleasant Prussian castle, Wilhelmshöhe, north of Frankfurt[85].

---

[85] Incidentally, one of the many Franco-Prussian skirmishes that took place before Napoléon III was captured was the Battle of

On September 4, a Parisian mob invaded the Palais Bourbon, the parliament building by the Seine, and radical MPs declared a new Republic. A crowd gathered outside the Palais des Tuileries, rattling the railings and chanting 'Vive la République!'

Fearing for her life, Eugénie packed a few bags and fled into exile in England – wearing a simple, anonymous black outfit. It wasn't the right time to dress up in one of Worth's eye-catching creations. In stark contrast to her recent trip to Egypt, she was, of course, obliged to travel light, and had to abandon all the as yet unworn Worth outfits stored in the vast wardrobe above her dressing room at the Palace.

※※※

As the rioters took control of the Paris streets and news spread that the Second Empire was at an end, Charles and Marie Worth knew that there would be no more summons to the Tuileries to discuss new ball gowns. They heard that Pauline von Metternich had fled with her children to London, and that many of their other faithful customers were not waiting around in Paris to see exactly how badly-behaved the mobs would get.

Having lived through the city's previous uprising in 1848, Charles and Marie knew all too well that revolution brings recession. The prospects for their 1870-71 winter

---

Wörth (with an umlaut) on 6 August 1870, named after a village in the northeast of France. It resulted in almost all the 15,000-odd French troops either dying, being captured or going missing. Suddenly the word 'Worth' must have taken on unpleasant connotations in French minds.

season were not good.

Demonstrators began to rip down shop signs that boasted 'by appointment to Her Imperial Majesty the Empress.' Worth et Bobergh was a well-known purveyor to the old regime, so 7 rue de la Paix was a prime target.

The Worths must have wondered whether to empty their safe, grab Charles's best cutting scissors, and follow Eugénie and Pauline across the Channel.

15 ANARCHY IN THE CITY

For the moment, Charles and Marie decided not to abandon Paris. They had put together a winning team of specialized French seamstresses and a highly trained local sales staff. Their suppliers of lace and many other fabrics were in France. Despite Charles's original nationality, their reputation was built on being *très parisien*. It would be impossible, and probably unprofitable, to start again from scratch in England. So they simply closed up shop and awaited political and military developments.

Charles announced that he would not be creating any new dresses for the autumn-winter season. Bravely, one of his faithful aristocratic clients, the Marquise Josefa de Manzanedo, announced that she would wear his muslin summer dresses through the winter as a gesture of support. According to Jean-Philippe Worth, when a friend asked her about this, she replied: 'Paris is closed. Worth is closed. How can I have any new dresses made?' Not that there were many social occasions now that most of high society had left town.

Otto Bobergh apparently saw no future in the Paris fashion business. He decided to go home to Sweden. Charles gave Otto his half of the profits, and the partnership was dissolved.

From now on, if the company survived, it would be officially known as La Maison Worth.

ʊʊʊ

The Worths received reassuring news about Eugénie – she had made it to England. What was more, a large number of Charles's creations had been sent after her.

This was thanks to a loyal imperialist by the name of Maurice d'Irisson d'Hérisson, an officer in Paris's new military command. At great personal risk, Hérisson went into Eugénie's private apartments at the Palais des Tuileries soon after she fled, on a mission to save as many as possible of the Empress's private possessions.

In his journal[86], he notes the tasteful décor in the Empress's (as yet un-looted) *salons* and bedroom, then goes upstairs to the floor where her clothes were stored. Here he finds 'an arsenal' of garments worthy of a 'supremely attractive woman who knows that beauty is a force and that, as our forefathers sang, art enhances beauty.'

Hérisson is stupefied to find 'a hat room, a boot room, a fur room' and a row of wardrobes 'packed with dresses of all sorts, coats, petticoats, a supply of underclothes, lacework, lengths of fabric and a considerable stock of rolls of Chinese silks.' He also describes four fully-dressed mannequins 'of her Majesty's exact height and size', decked out in what Eugénie had certainly planned to wear on the day she fled.

As Hérisson searched for items that the refugee Empress might need, he could hear 'the great roar of the

---

[86] *Journal d'un officier d'ordonnance: Juillet 1870-février 1871*, by Maurice d'Irisson d'Hérisson, published in 1885.

whole population outside, a rumble punctuated from time to time by cries of "Vive la République!" shouted by youths, or snippets of the Marseillaise carried on the breeze from the crossroads and the riverbanks.' He knew that the mob might break in at any moment.

With the help of one of the Empress's ladies-in-waiting who had stayed on, Hérisson packed fifteen trunks with clothes and accessories and had them taken to the Gare du Nord, and sent from there to England. A few days later he received a thank-you note sent from the Marine Hotel, Hastings. Out of concern for Hérisson's safety, Eugénie did not sign it, but he recognized the handwriting. She said, 'I must be brief here, but my heart feels no less for that.'

A newcomer to the female fashion industry, Hérisson did not save exclusively Worth dresses, but he certainly kitted Eugénie out with a generous number of her favourite designer's creations to wear during her exile.

ʊʊʊ

As September 1870 dragged on, the news about the war became increasingly alarming. With Napoléon III a prisoner and most of his army either captured or besieged inside the city of Metz (on French territory), the Prussians demanded immediate surrender. Unsurprisingly, the Parisian revolutionary government gave a less-than-polite reply, with the new Minister of Foreign Affairs Jules Favre declaring that they would yield 'not one inch[87] of our territory or one stone of our fortresses.'

---

[87] Favre used the word *pouce* – meaning inch. France had still not gone wholly metric. By the way, 'stones' here obviously does not refer to an imperial measure of weight; Favre used the word *pierres*, and was talking about the stones used in construction of the fortresses.

The Prussian army proceeded to march almost unchallenged towards Paris, grabbing countless inches and stones as it went, in a 19th century precursor to Blitzkrieg. By 19 September, Paris was surrounded and the siege of the city began.

Retreating French soldiers poured into Paris, and Charles and Marie turned their premises into a makeshift military hospital. Many of their permanent staff, none of whom were laid off despite the lack of business, became nurses and medical orderlies. Jean-Philippe recalled that: 'We took cases of pneumonia, dysentery and all the diseases that follow in the path of war, and were greatly saddened by the death of several soldiers committed to our care hopelessly ill. It was a dreadful time.'

With Prussian troops encamped all around the city, the Worths could not get to their out-of-town house. Worryingly for them, the Château de Saint-Cloud, one of the imperial homes where Charles's dresses had been shown off to their greatest effect, was occupied by the enemy. On 13 October it was fired on by French cannons and destroyed. This was three kilometres south of Suresnes. Five days later, there was a pitched battle (which the French lost) in Rueil-Malmaison, just three kilometres west of the *château Worth*. The likelihood that things would ever get back to normal seemed slim.

ϖϖϖ

The invaders were determined to starve the Parisians into submission. At first, the small urban farms within the siege line (in Montmartre, for example) provided fresh provisions of vegetables, dairy produce and meat. As well-off citizens, the Worths probably had access to decent food for longer than most – we can't know for sure, because Jean-Philippe gives almost no details about their life during this time. But we know that ordinary Parisians soon became desperate.

Any horse or mule not needed for the war effort was slaughtered. Household pets were sacrificed and *le chien* became a Frenchman's best friend in a new, culinary way. A newspaper, *Le Quotidien des Nouvelles (Daily News)*, published a list of siege recipes including dog cutlets with peas, cat's back with mayonnaise, rat salami, and an alternative for cream – horse marrow *jus*.

These were not just idle suggestions. In the Musée Carnavalet, Paris's history museum, there is a painting of a young rat butcher with a furry rodent on his chopping block. The price tag: two francs, which was the daily wage of one of the Worths' less qualified seamstresses. Rat had become an expensive delicacy.

In the same museum there is a collection of plates wittily illustrated with scenes from the siege. One of them depicts a bourgeois household: a lady weeps into her handkerchief as the man of the house stares thoughtfully at a cute labrador-type dog that is sitting obediently, gazing lovingly up at its master. Canine cutlets will soon be on the menu.

Another plate shows a street scene in which a cat is about to pounce on a rat, little knowing that a man is creeping up behind it with a club in his hand. This was Paris's new food chain.

A third shows a portly grocer pointing proudly at a display of un-labelled cans. At his feet behind the counter, hidden from the hungry-looking shoppers, a cat is standing by a large mousehole. The grocer's smile says it all: come and play the tinned-meat lottery.

Restaurants began to sell nameless stews, and the poet Victor Hugo admitted that he often did not know what was on his plate: 'We're not eating horse anymore.

Perhaps it's dog? Perhaps it's rat? I'm starting to get stomach aches. We're eating the unknown.'

The only animal off the menu was modern Paris's airborne pest, the pigeon. Carrier pigeons were vital for conveying messages across the siege lines, so to prevent an army messenger accidentally being turned into a fricassee, the death penalty was imposed for anyone killing a pigeon. For the same reason, in Prussian-occupied territory, any French person keeping pigeons could be shot. It was the 1870 equivalent of the Nazis' ban on radios.

The animals at the Paris Zoo were not safe for very long. In October 1870, barely a month after the start of the siege, the keepers began slaughtering deer, zebra, buffaloes and yaks, before moving on to less conventional meats such as elephant trunk (at 40 francs per pound). The zoo animals were all gone by the end of the year. The Christmas 1870 dinner at the Café Voisin in the rue Saint Honoré, a ten-minute stroll from the rue de la Paix, accounted for quite a few of them. Its chef, Alexandre Choron, served up elephant consommé, camel roasted *à l'anglaise* (meaning without sauce), wolf thighs in deer gravy, truffle and antelope pâté, bear ribs in a pepper sauce, kangaroo stew and cat garnished with rats (and, to make it more palatable, a watercress salad). Apart from that last dish, this was a dinner aimed at the ultra-rich. We do not know if the Worths attended, but there were probably a few of Charles's dresses on show in the Café Voisin that night.

ϖϖϖ

In his memoirs, Jean-Philippe Worth says that one positive thing came out of the siege, thanks to his parents' friend, the painter Camille Corot, then an old man of 74 but at the height of his fame. Corot came from the same background as the Worths. His family had run a fabric shop on the corner of the rue du Bac and quai Voltaire, just opposite the Louvre. In 1815 Corot's father sent the young Camille to be an apprentice with a draper's in the rue de Richelieu, before the budding painter convinced his parents to let him pursue a career in art. His affinity with the Worths was natural.

During the siege of 1870-71, Corot would come to the rue de la Paix to share whatever food they had all been able to buy, and the painter offered to give Jean-Philippe, then 14, art lessons[88]. The boy was not an attentive pupil at school, and was often told off for doodling when he should have been writing, so weekly lessons with the famous artist were a dream come true, and would prepare him for a career at La Maison Worth, first as an assistant to his father (as of 1874), then as a designer.

But these art lessons on a Sunday were rare moments of pleasure in a life that was becoming increasingly dour. As the siege dragged on, food became so scarce that even rat doubled and then tripled in price. Rationing was introduced. There were huge queues outside food shops. What bread there was available contained more and more straw instead of flour. Most of the population of Paris, both male and female, was mobilized to fight, but all attempts to break through the Prussian lines failed, and the invaders started to shoot anyone who left the city, even if they were only scavenging for food.

In January 1871, Bismarck lost his patience and began bombarding Paris. During a continuous day-and-

---

[88] This was typical of Corot's generosity. In 1871 he donated 20,000 francs to help feed poor Parisians.

night barrage, Prussian cannons destroyed houses, schools, churches and hospitals at random. Parisians remembered with some bitterness how they had admired these very same Krupp guns at the *Exposition Universelle* of 1867.

Finally an armistice was negotiated, and the Prussians agreed to a symbolic occupation of Paris: on 1 March 1871, they were to take over little more than a corridor either side of the Champs-Elysées, with French troops preventing any incursions further afield. The victors held a triumphal parade through the Arc de Triomphe, and then for two days, slightly bemused Prussian soldiers wandered the litter-strewn streets in their occupied sector, no doubt wondering where Paris had got its reputation as a chic party town. The city was silent and almost empty. This was because, as a gesture of resistance, Parisians closed all their shops, shut all their shutters and totally ignored the occupiers.

The invaders left, as agreed, and the Franco-Prussian War was over. Fresh food started to arrive in Paris again – as did letters containing orders for new dresses. The Worths' foreign customers seemed to be especially pleased that France had re-opened for business. Charles and Marie assembled their staff and prepared their workshops for a relaunch after their enforced six-month closure.

But the Parisians had other ideas …

16 THINGS CAN ONLY GET WORSE

Even as Prussian troops were retreating home to Germany, France held parliamentary elections and, although it was now nominally a republic, the voters elected King Louis-Philippe's former Minister of the Interior as President. This was 73-year-old Adolphe Thiers, a rich royalist who chose to re-locate parliament outside Paris, in Versailles, the traditional home of French kings[89].

This snub was too much for the Parisians, who in March 1871 revolted, barricaded the streets and more or less declared independence. It was the start of what became known as the Commune, one of the bloodiest episodes of civil war in France's turbulent history.

In an act of deliberate mischief, the Prussians released 60,000 French prisoners of war and left their new Krupp cannons behind, so that Thiers suddenly had his army back again, with artillery conveniently pointed at Paris.

At this point, a large proportion of better-off Parisians decided they had had enough. The upper and

---

[89] For a full analysis of France's tendency to revert to a form of royalism at almost every opportunity between 1789 and 1871, see my book, *The French Revolution & What Went Wrong*.

middle classes left town, and civil servants joined the government in Versailles. The Worths stayed on – at first.

ʊʊʊ

The American letter-writer Madame Moulton visited 7 rue de la Paix on March 21, and almost died for it. She had spent the war in Dinard, in Brittany, and returned to Paris once the armistice had been announced, only to find the city in the hands of what she calls 'impertinent, common-looking' men brandishing bayonets and threatening anyone rich – Madame Moulton in her carriage, for instance. At one point, a Communard tried to 'liberate' her horse for the people.

She deposited her luggage at her home in the chic rue de Courcelles, in the west of the city, and then bravely went out to explore. She found the rue de la Paix barricaded, and finished her journey on foot. But no sooner had she been welcomed in by the Worths than they heard 'distant, confused sounds' and 'shouting in the street.' She, Charles and Marie went out on to the balcony to investigate. 'What a sight met our eyes!' she says.

Madame Moulton had previously heard about 'a young fellow called Henri de Pène[90]' campaigning for peace on behalf of ordinary, peace-loving Parisians. She says that he was trying to rally support for a march to the barricade in the Place Vendôme (at the end of the rue de la Paix) 'in order to beg the Communards, in the name

---

[90] This may well have been Henry (with a Y) de Pène, a journalist at *Le Figaro* newspaper. If so, Madame Moulton is wrong when she says that he was killed in the rue de la Paix. Henry de Pène survived until 1888.

of the people, to restore order and quiet in the city. He sent word beforehand to say that they would come there *unarmed.*' (Her italics).

His procession arrived in the area at almost exactly the same time as Madame Moulton, and the 'distant, confused sounds' she heard were the chants of de Pène's protesters. 'This mass of humanity walked down the rue de la Paix, filling the whole breadth of it.' They looked up as they passed number 7, and beckoned Charles to join them. But 'Mister Worth wisely withdrew inside and, shaking his Anglo-Saxon head, said "Not I." '

Almost immediately, a cannon shot rang out, and 'frightened screams and terrified groans reached our ears.' The street was suddenly full of smoke, corpses and fleeing protesters.

Terrified, Madame Moulton was desperate to escape. One of the Worths' employees took her into the next building, via an adjoining door in the upstairs workshops. The American bribed the concierge with a gold piece to let her out the back entrance into the street, found her driver (easily: he was the only man in sight wearing gloves) and hurried home, 'my legs trembling, my head swimming and my heart sick.'

Meanwhile, the Worths had courageously opened their doors to the fleeing protesters. According to Jean-Philippe, about 300 took refuge there, including some of the wounded, at least one of whom died in the shop. Charles ferried the others out to safety into the rue Volney, the street running parallel to the rue de la Paix behind La Maison Worth.

Charles and Marie realized that business was not going to return to normal any time soon. And when the Communards tried to force their elder son Gaston (then aged 17) to join their army, the family decided to escape.

'We had to quit the house in the rue de la Paix separately,' Jean-Philippe wrote, 'so as not to arouse suspicion, and met at the Gare Saint Lazare where we took a train for [Le] Havre.' This was, of course, just across the Channel from England. Charles had always kept his British passport, and was ready to move his family to safety in case the situation in France became really threatening.

※※※

They were wise to leave Paris. The city descended into bloody chaos as the Versailles-based government army attacked. This was an age of early photography, so there are plenty of surviving pictures of smashed barricades, corpse-strewn streets, and even close-ups of bullet-riddled Communards executed by the government troops. The vengeful Versailles troops were led by Marshal Patrice de MacMahon, who had suffered defeat at the Battle of Sedan alongside Napoléon III, and was in no mood to be humiliated again.

According to the city of Paris's website, *Paris.fr*, by the end of the so-called '*semaine sanglante*' (bloody week) of 21-28 May 1871, during which MacMahon's army stormed 900 Parisian barricades, between 3,000 and 5,000 Communard soldiers had been killed in battle. About 20,000 more were captured and massacred, often mown down with machine guns. Some 43,000 civilians – men, women and children – were arrested and put into an insanitary prison camp in Satory, near Versailles, with no shelter and little food. Many would die there of disease, dozens were executed, and almost 4,000 would be deported to penal colonies in the tropics. On the opposing side, between 500 and 800 government troops died fighting, with 5,000 more wounded. Figures are vague because of the anarchy reigning at the time, as well as cover-ups. For example, it wasn't until 1897 that a mass grave of 800 Communards was unearthed in Charonne, in the north of Paris.

As well as the tragic human cost, the city suffered some sad architectural losses too. The Communards burned down City Hall – the Hôtel de Ville. They tried to torch the Louvre but were prevented by government troops. They did manage to pull barrels of tar and gunpowder into the Palais des Tuileries, before lighting the fuses and watching the imperial palace explode. It had already been looted, but there may well have been a few of Charles Worth's creations in the inferno.

ωωω

Once the street battles and massacres were over, the Worths returned from Le Havre. Their home was still intact, but the streets of Paris were piled with debris – practically every cobblestone had been ripped up to build barricades – and when they walked to the Tuileries, they got a terrible shock. All that was left of the palace where their career had been launched was a skeleton of bare, blackened walls. Marie wept on Charles's arm. He slumped into despair. The glory days of the Second Empire really had gone up in smoke.

17 NEW BEGINNINGS

In August 1871, a British journalist, F. Adolphus, decided to interview France's most famous English resident. As he recalled in his memoir, *Some Memories of Paris*[91]: 'I had been told that he was as busy as a Cabinet Minister; that it was more difficult to obtain an audience from him than from a reigning sovereign; that he was a loftier personage, by far, than any living poet.'

But Adolphus was determined to get Charles Worth's views on recent political events in France. He saw the fashion designer as something of an oracle: 'I often heard the Second Empire described as "l'époque de Worth." In such a position, he surely owed himself to the world, especially to humble inquirers like myself who sought simply to sit at his feet and listen to his words of wisdom.'

Adolphus motivated himself with the thought that Worth's 'personality was too great, too dominating, too full of public responsibilities, to permit him to refuse to enlighten his generation on such a virgin question as the connection between frocks and battles.'

So the journalist went to the rue de la Paix[92] and had

---

[91] Published in 1895.
[92] He says it was number 5 but this was presumably a mistake. Or an early example of fake news.

his visiting card taken to the great man. Five minutes later, Worth received him, and Adolphus explained that he wanted to write 'an article on the influence of the war on the dressmaking trade [...] You typify, for everybody, the entire idea of Paris dressmaking.'

Initially, Worth, a businessman more than a philosopher, was bemused: 'He stared curiously (perhaps rather suspiciously) at me,' before replying that he was too busy now: 'At this instant seventeen persons are waiting for me in nine rooms. Come to dine with me at my country house. Take the 6.30 train from St Lazare to Suresnes. My son will meet you at the station and show you the way. À demain.'

Adolphus was over the moon. 'The great man' had agreed to his request, 'not only benignly but with a cordiality that filled me with hopes.'

Next day, Adolphus was greeted at the station by Gaston Worth, and they chatted amiably as they walked up to the house. A few minutes later, 'I heard the gallop of a horse tearing up the hill and Mr. Worth, spattered with mud and foam, rode in at the gate.' Charles often used to ride to Suresnes on horseback, making the most of the fresh air after spending the whole day in the suffocating atmosphere of his fitting rooms.

While Charles changed, Adolphus was introduced to Marie, about whom he also had strong pre-conceived views. He was, somewhat patronizingly, expecting to meet a former shopgirl with airs and graces: 'I had heard that Madame Worth, with the adaptability of many of her race, had fitted herself admirably to her new situation, and had become in everything a lady.' He was favourably impressed: 'With the ease of an accomplished woman of the world, with combined dignity and simplicity, with infinite gentleness of movement, she made two steps towards me, smiling graciously, bowing slightly, welcome on her face.' He apparently had no idea that Marie had been meeting and greeting the haughtiest people in Europe for more than twenty years. She was the head of public relations for one of France's most successful companies, and this journalist was another potentially useful person for the Worth brand. *Of course* she knew how to greet him with effortless graciousness.

Adolphus did not suspect it, but perhaps Charles and Marie were conscious that their business was still teetering after its close brush with catastrophe. A good write-up in the British press was exactly what they needed. This was probably why Charles had ridden from the shop at top speed to be on time for the interview.

Marie had even dressed up, and Adolphus was spellbound: 'She wore a high but short-sleeved white satin dress, striped with bands of black velvet; a profusion of lace hung over her; long suede gloves reached almost to her shoulders; two or three bracelets were on her arms; a diamond was half hidden here and there in the lace [...] All other women in white satin appeared to me impostors.'

While they waited, Marie made small-talk, or so Adolphus seems to have thought. In fact, it sounds as though she was very much in professional mode. She asked him 'in a soft voice, "I hear you want Mr. Worth to give you information about the effect of the siege upon our business. He will be very pleased to do so, and I hope you will let me read what you write about it." ' Marie was clearly going to make sure that the journalist printed only what the Worths approved.

After that, conversation dried up. Adolphus consoled himself that Marie was being shy – 'the delightful woman was a little silent' – but she was probably just being businesslike. She must have known that it was unwise to be too chatty with a reporter.

Charles joined them, informally dressed in a rusty brown jacket and a battered straw hat, and they all dined in 'a vast greenhouse that seemed to cover an acre of surface', with a few of Marie's provincial relatives – 'some quiet persons, who did not speak' – they, it seems, had also received instructions not to be indiscreet. After soup Charles told the writer, 'Now put your queries. I am ready.'

Adolphus confessed that he wanted to write about more than the war: he was interested in 'the metaphysical aspects of dressmaking.'

Charles steered him back to the subject at hand: 'The war has done me harm, of course [...] I have lost a year by it; but I daresay I shall pick up again, for orders are coming in very fast.'

Adolphus persisted: 'With what object do women dress?', and Charles took up the gauntlet, proceeding to give him probably the fullest and most honest account of his craft that was ever written down. Here are some key excerpts from a long and fascinating masterclass that Adolphus transcribed with either miraculous recall or an exceptional gift for shorthand. Charles explained that:

> Women dress, of course, for two reasons: for the pleasure of making themselves smart, and for the still greater joy of snuffing out others.'
>
> 'The women who come to me want to ask for my ideas, not to follow their own. They deliver themselves to me in confidence, and I decide for them; that makes them happy.'

'My business is not only to execute but especially to invent. My invention is the secret of my success. I don't want people to invent for themselves. If they did, I should lose half of my trade.'

'There are quantities of very respectable women in Paris who don't spend more than £60[93] a year on their toilet, and who, for that sort of type, really don't look bad. But the women who come to me are of a different class. Well, they get through anything from a minimum of £400 to a maximum of £4,000 [...] Why, some of them – especially the Russians – need £150 a year for shoes alone, without counting boots [...] The French are usually rather careful; economy is in the blood, you know [...] But rarely does an Englishwoman get really wasteful, and I have not known a single case of a German reaching any such amount as I am talking of. Some of the Americans are great spenders; all of them that I see [...] love dress, even if they are not extravagant over it. And I like to dress them for, as I say occasionally, "they have faith, figures and francs" – faith to believe in me, figures that I can put into shape, francs to pay my bills. Yes, I like to dress Americans.'

[Adolphus asks whether trade will pick up quickly after the siege and Charles

---

[93] In 1870, £1 sterling was worth roughly 25 francs, or about ten days' of an average seamstress's wages. So Worth is quoting enormous prices for his outfits, making Paris sound very extravagant.

replies:] 'Oh certainly. I haven't a doubt about it. Women can't do without new clothes: they may deprive themselves of all sorts of other things, but they won't shut off that one. They can't. I'm quite sure that, by the end of the year, we shall be going on as if nothing had happened. Payments will be, for a time, more difficult to get in – French payments, I mean; foreign payments are not affected by the war – but trade itself will become as active as ever.'

'It is precisely the unnecessary and the frivolous that everyone comes to buy in Paris. People don't travel from everywhere to the boulevards to lay in stocks of timber.'

'The war will bring about no permanent change in women's wants. The future will be like the past, excepting, of course that (unless there is a Restoration of some sort) there will be, from the disappearance of a court, less brilliancy in Paris itself, and less demand here for extreme elegance. So far as I am concerned, however, I expect that foreign orders will make up for what I lose here.'

Surprisingly, Adolphus declares to his readers that he was exasperated by all this pontificating, and hadn't got the answers he needed. He admits that he didn't bother transcribing more than another hour's worth of racy anecdotes about famous clients and strange goings-on in the fitting room, of which Charles naively told him, 'They are confidential, you know.'

Adolphus tells Worth that scurrilous stories like that would not interest British readers (the UK press has obviously changed a lot since then). And in the end, he never wrote his article. Instead, he saved it to fill almost twenty pages of his memoirs.

The Worths were probably disappointed that nothing came of the interview. Charles had certainly delivered an excellent piece of self-publicity.

Interestingly, at one point early in the discussion, when Charles seemed to be faltering on the subject of women's motivations for buying expensive dresses, Marie tried to pitch in and help: 'I suspect I know more about all that than my husband does.'

This piqued Charles's ego: 'Ah, but it is I, not you, who am being examined [...] and I mean to keep the answering to myself.' And from then he doesn't let up. His reply could be seen as an example of a domineering 19th century male silencing his presumptuous wife. Or maybe Marie was wielding what we now call soft power: the canny publicist knowing exactly how to goad her hesitant company spokesman into delivering the required message.

ʊʊʊ

It was true that business had picked up. Soon after the new government was installed in Paris, the President's wife, Élise Thiers, ordered new dresses for the receptions that were to be held at the Elysée Palace. However, in contrast to Eugénie's glittering white gowns for her official occasions, Madame Thiers wanted black, with few trimmings. She had never been a fan of the extravagance of the Second Empire. Pauline von Metternich knew her and said that Madame Thiers always ignored current fashions and 'gave the impression of protesting against what she called the corruption of the Empire.' (This was somewhat ironic, as Élise was in fact the daughter of Adolphe Thiers' mistress.) In any case, it did not seem likely that the women of the new presidential entourage would be knocking on the Worths' door at dawn to order a ball gown.

There was a glimmer of hope that glamorous nightlife might flourish again when the Metternichs returned to their ambassadorial residence in Paris. However, President Thiers immediately asked Vienna to replace them because they had been too closely linked with Napoléon and Eugénie. The couple left in January 1872, depriving the Worths of orders for countless party dresses.

Fortunately, now that peace was established in Paris, tourists began to return, and on arrival, many of the women jumped in a carriage and drove to the Maison Worth. The diarist Edmond de Goncourt noted this in his entry for 11 January 1872: 'Recently, finding the rue de la Paix blocked by a line of stylish carriages, just like a first night at the Théâtre Français, I wondered which great celebrity was being besieged by the greats of this world. Then, lifting my gaze above an entrance porch, I read: "Worth." Paris is still the Paris of the Empire.'

That was something of an exaggeration, but just as in 1789 and 1848, it was true that fashion had outlived a revolution, and the reputation of Charles Worth, the unrivalled star of the Second Empire, had not faded.

In May 1873, with the election as President of Patrice MacMahon, the man who had so brutally suppressed the Commune, a new court was founded.

Despite being the head of the Third Republic, MacMahon was an old-school monarchist. He chose as Prime Minister (*Président du conseil des ministres*) Albert de Broglie, an aristocrat and former supporter of King

Louis-Philippe. Together, MacMahon and Broglie planned to restore the French royal family to power[94]. Even Napoléon III himself had ambitions of returning to France from his British exile and reviving his Empire, but in January 1873, he died after a botched operation for kidney stones performed by an English surgeon.[95]

In any case, MacMahon and his ministers restored Paris's glittering social scene. There were presidential dinners, balls and state receptions. Mathilde Bonaparte came back to Paris and started up her *salons* again. All of this was excellent news for La Maison Worth.

ಐಐಐ

In 1878 Paris hosted another *Exposition Universelle*, a great international occasion at which the head of the Statue of Liberty was unveiled (the completed sculpture would be inaugurated in New York in 1886).

One of the most prestigious visitors to this *Expo* was Princess Alexandra, the wife of the future King Edward VII. She came in person to the rue de la Paix for a fitting, which did not go as well as those with previous princesses. Alexandra was deaf, and was attended by three ladies-in-waiting who fussed around and would not stop warning Charles's fitter against sticking pins into Her Majesty.

According to Jean-Philippe, the fitter 'dripped with perspiration and trembled with nervousness,' but Alexandra remained blissfully unaware of the uproar going on around her.

---

[94] For the reasons why this did not eventually happen, see my book *The French Revolution & What Went Wrong*.
[95] Tales like this still encourage modern French expats to return home to France from Britain for any major medical intervention.

ඟඟඟ

Meanwhile, as Charles had told the journalist Adolphus, his attention was increasingly turning away from Paris.

With foreign orders rolling in, Charles began to gain more confidence about the future. He must have realized that in a way he, like France itself, had shrugged off the chains of an authoritarian regime. He no longer had to wait for the Empress or one of her entourage to wear a new style of garment before it became 'acceptable'. In the past, even though he had bullied individual clients into wearing what he told them to, he had often had to accept that he was just an influencer on trends; Eugénie usually took the final decision. Now he could be the absolute dictator of fashion. He had customers all over the world who hung on his every word and gesture.

In New York, the young novelist Henry James was actively promoting the idea that chic American girls *had* to wear Paris fashions. In his first novel, *Watch and Ward*, published in 1871, a young woman called Nora comes of age when 'one fine day she was eighteen and sported a black silk dress of Paris!' She says she is spending an ideal summer: 'I go to balls and wear Paris dresses.'

Rich Americans took note, and La Maison Worth's *haute couture* client list expanded with names like Carnegie, Astor, Rockefeller, Whitney and Vanderbilt. One of the most faithful, and richest, of these transatlantic customers was the banker John Pierpoint (alias J.P.) Morgan, who had helped to finance France's recovery after the Franco-Prussian War and the Commune. Morgan brought his wife Frances to the rue de la Paix in 1877, and even insisted on attending fittings himself. Not, apparently, because he had read Zola and Larousse and feared for Mrs. Morgan's morals, but because he enjoyed discussing the finer points of fashion with the master of the trade.

Whenever J.P. Morgan came over to Paris on business without his family, he would drop in to see Charles and order new dresses – naturally, Worth had Mrs. Morgan's measurements on file. As well as enjoying pleasant conversations with the highly civilized American, Charles appreciated the fact that Morgan's bills were never questioned and always swiftly paid.

Soon the name of Worth was so famous that it was a social necessity to know about him in the USA.

The American author Frances Hodgson Burnett, best known for *The Secret Garden*, wrote a novel called *Louisiana* in 1880. In it, a New York socialite, Miss Ferrol, hopes to adopt a good-looking young country girl called Louisiana as her *protegée*, and tests her general knowledge. She enquires whether the girl knows the philosopher John Stuart Mill (no), the art critic John Ruskin (no), Michelangelo ('I think so, but I don't know what he did'). In despair Miss Ferrol asks, enunciating her words very slowly, 'Do-you-know-anything-about-Worth?' When the poor girl answers 'no, nothing', the socialite shrieks with horror: 'How you have been neglected.'[96]

Even if the scene was meant to be ironic, Worth was being mentioned in the same breath as the great names of the age, as well as a Renaissance demi-god. And when Louisiana tries on a Worth dress (that Miss Ferrol looks at 'religiously'), the narrator is genuinely impressed: 'The lovely young figure was revealed in all its beauty of outline.'

---

[96] Chapter two of the novel, entitled simply 'Worth', is devoted to Louisiana's first encounter with Charles's dresses.

As time went on, more and more of La Maison Worth's trade involved shipping product abroad. Before 1870, Charles and Marie had often been able to observe their dresses *in situ*, relishing the way Eugénie, Pauline or some other socialite attracted admiration for a unique Worth creation at a Parisian event. Now, Charles would often conduct a sitting with a tourist who would leave town before her gown was even finished. He would inspect the finished garment, and then watch it being taken away for packaging.

Many of his clients, like J.P. Morgan's wife, could have a dress made without coming anywhere near the rue de la Paix. There is an example in Edith Wharton's novel *The Age of Innocence,* which was published in 1920, but described American life in the 1870s. In it, Wharton describes a customer of Worth's called Mrs Baxter Penilow who: 'used to import twelve [dresses] a year, two velvet, two satin, two silk and the other six of poplin and the finest cashmere. It was a standing order, and as she was ill for two years before she died, they found forty-eight Worth dresses that had never been taken out of tissue paper.'

This was a radical change in customer relations, proof that La Maison Worth was taking a lead role in yet another innovation in the world of fashion.

18 PRÊT À PORTER

Some of the 19th century's most memorable, and yet least practical, inventions originated in France: can-can dancing, Impressionism, the Statue of Liberty, the Eiffel Tower (though that did come in useful as a radio aerial). But one French innovation from that period is so handy that it is still used by hundreds of millions of people all over the world today. That is the department store.

In French, the department store is known, even more literally than in English, as a *grand magasin* – a 'big shop'. Its size was always its main selling point.

It evolved out of a type of store that was known as a *magasin de nouveautés* – this did not mean novelties in the sense of gadgets or trinkets, but new fashions in fabrics and (later) ready-made clothing.

In the early 19th century, when many women made, mended or altered their own clothes, the *magasins de nouveautés* flourished all over Paris, and attracted customers with their lively shop window displays, low prices, and general lack of snobbishness.

In France, and especially in Paris, when the Second Empire began to create not only wider prosperity but also a heightened taste for fashion and showiness amongst the burgeoning middle classes, the *magasins de nouveautés* boomed. They were so successful that some of their owners saw the potential for expansion – on a grandiose scale.

It is generally accepted that Le Bon Marché (the 'good market', and *'bon marché'* also means inexpensive), just south of the Quartier Latin, was the first Parisian *grand magasin*. It was originally founded in its smallest form in 1838, with 12 staff in four departments selling sewing articles, mattresses, sheets and umbrellas. It expanded in 1853, taking its commercial innovations several stages further: the range of stock was broadened, and this economy of scale enabled the shop to offer more competitive prices, which were written on price tags, reducing the embarrassment of asking 'c'est combien?'.

Another big name that still exists today, Le Printemps ('spring'), was opened in 1865 on the Boulevard Haussmann, a five-minute carriage trot from the rue de la Paix. It was initially called Les Grands Magasins du Printemps (the 'big shops of spring'). The new store adopted the commercial principles of the Bon Marché and added its own novelties: these included periodic sales to clear out unsold stock, and mannequins in shop windows.[97]

There are only a few other survivors from the early crop of Parisian *grands magasins* – the Galeries Lafayette, La Samaritaine[98] and the BHV (Bazaar de l'Hôtel de Ville). But in the mid to late 19th century almost every

---

[97] Later, the Bon Marché introduced perhaps the most important reason for visiting a department store in 19th-century Paris: ladies' toilets.

[98] Originally called Les Grands Magasins de la Samaritaine, it was named after a nearby drinking-water pump that was decorated with sculptures representing the Good Samaritan episode from the Bible.

quartier of Paris boasted its department store, often named after its location. These included: À la Place Clichy, Aux Phares de la Bastille, Aux Buttes Chaumont and Chaussée Clignancourt. The literalness of their names was part of their direct marketing. The same can be said, of course, for Le Bon Marché.

Their creation – or expansion – coincided with Baron Haussmann's rebuilding of the city, so they were usually housed in new, purpose-built constructions. Like their products, they needed to exude modernity, so that iron beams and staircases, or daring glass domes, like the Galeries Lafayette's famous cupola, were *de rigueur*. Ceilings on the ground floors were high, creating huge exhibition spaces, much like those that Parisians had seen at the *Expositions Universelles* of 1855 and 1867. These were retail palaces, cathedrals to consumerism.

At their zenith, the *grands magasins* employed squadrons of staff in a dizzying array of departments. In the 1870s, for example, Le Bon Marché had about 2,500 sales assistants, plus all those who worked in admin, shipping and the kitchens. The departments relevant to women's clothing (*excluding* shoes, hats and accessories) were: ladies' suits, ladies' jackets, ladies' coats, petticoats, dressing gowns, corsets, fashions, lace, Lyons lace, ribbons, cottons, embroidery, coloured wools, 'fantasy wools', black wools, coloured silks, black silks, and Indian fabrics. These were all individual departments, each with a dozen or more sales staff. Interestingly, the sections dealing purely with fabrics were usually staffed by men. Saleswomen were restricted to departments where female customers might want to try garments on.

When Émile Zola was researching *Au Bonheur des Dames* (often translated into English as *The Ladies' Paradise*, the name of a fictitious store), his 1882 novel about the creation of the *grands magasins*, he estimated that these 'Babylonian palaces' employed about ten per cent of Parisian males, most of them under 35. They, their female colleagues and the *petites mains* we saw earlier brought vibrant activity to the boulevards during the day and after work, enhancing Paris's reputation as a lively place to be.

ϖϖϖ

These department stores are rightly credited with revolutionizing, or at least industrializing, retail practices. But the Worths had already started using some of the same methods.

It was only natural that there should be some cross-pollination: the *grands magasins* and Worth et Bobergh were expanding at the same time. Gagelin was a chic *magasin de nouveautés*, and Charles and Marie had begun developing their future business practices from that model, as the department stores did. More or less simultaneously, both the Worths and the first *grands magasins* saw the advantages of bringing different departments under one roof so that customers could be enticed away from visiting other shops. And Charles Worth began labelling his clothes with his brand so that he would stand out against all competitors, not only other *haute couture* dressmakers but also the *grands magasins*.

However, the Worths seem to have been ahead of the department stores in some areas. The *grands magasins* published catalogues of spring-summer and autumn-winter fashions, imitating Worth's strategy of imposing seasonal styles; both ran mail-order services, including international deliveries, but Worth was sending out foreign orders very early in his career, before the *grands magasins* had developed that far.

The key similarity between Worth et Bobergh and the new department stores was that both were conscious of the need to perfect the customer experience. Au Printemps is celebrated by retail historians for handing out violets to its clients on the first day of spring, but (as we saw in Zola's *La Curée*) Worth's customers had been feasting on cakes and Madeira wine for years. And in making their establishments attractive-looking environments to shop in, with decorations that mimicked the interior of elegant bourgeois homes, the department stores were emulating the luxurious surroundings of pre-existing places like Gagelin and 7 rue de la Paix.

The *grands magasins*, like Worth, also knew that it was vital to play up their Parisian identity. Worth had famous clients who served as living adverts for his dresses in the theatres or at ceremonial occasions. The department stores could not make that claim, so they hired leading graphic artists to rival the best of Toulouse Lautrec's majestic advertisements for Paris's cabaret shows. Posters depicting elegant, seductive ladies appeared on billboards all over Paris and the provinces. Sophisticated women sported the latest fashions as they promenaded along the city's sunlit – or gaslit – boulevards. This was the Parisian dream, being sold at a bargain price.

ധധധ

Small shops naturally complained about unfair competition. Even high-end suppliers like Worth et Bobergh must have felt threatened by the department stores' offers of cheaper, luxury-style clothing. In 1869, a department store, Les Grands Magasins de la Paix, opened in what is now the rue du Quatre Septembre, just

300 metres from Worth et Bobergh. Its name was a blatant attempt to bathe in the aura of the rue de la Paix's reputation for quality. (However, it did not survive into the 20th century.)

In terms of the products on offer, Charles Worth probably viewed the department stores as portrait painters regarded the early photographers: there was undoubtedly a danger of losing some custom to this new-fangled invention.

On the other hand, a comparison between Worth's high-quality creations and the *grand magasins'* mass-produced outfits was more akin to matching Champagne against cheap sparkling wine. It was not exactly *competition*, because there was a proportion of the market that wanted *only* the real thing and nothing less. In addition, Worth was capable of designing for a mass market, whereas in his view the *grand magasins'* designers had neither the artistic talent nor the raw materials to produce anything truly worthy of La Maison Worth.

Even so, there was a real danger of unauthorized copies of his designs, or of imitations 'inspired by' his ideas, and Charles took measures to protect himself.

In 1868, he was the chief instigator behind the creation of a new professional body, La Chambre Syndicale de la Couture, des Confectionneurs et des Tailleurs pour Dames – literally a 'union chamber for sewing, dressmakers and ladies' tailors.'

The aim of this designers' guild was to defend the interests of, and give an official status to, genuine actors in France's fashion industry. If a dressmaker was not accepted by his or her peers as a member of the Chambre, he or she was not a genuine creator of that highly sought-after commodity: *la mode française*. In this way, cheap imitators could be named and shamed, and customers would know when they were buying the real thing.[99]

Typically, however, Charles Worth saw the new outlets as an opportunity. It was a case of 'if you can't beat them, join them'. Or rather, 'why not join them *and* beat them?'

After the Commune, despite the queue of carriages in the rue de la Paix described in the Goncourt diary, the Worths' business was already much less reliant than before on visits from high-society ladies. As we have seen, foreign orders started pouring in again as soon as the Prussian siege lines were dismantled. So, while Charles still offered his richest customers the full *haute couture* experience, with the master creating a unique work of art before their very eyes, he also decided to democratize the Worth brand. He began to move the business closer to the *grand magasin* model, making some of his designs available to the department stores – in effect creating an *haute couture* brand's first-ever *prêt à porter* ('ready to wear') line.

This is, of course, a business model that has since been adopted by almost every *haute couture* house since.

Charles had some of his dresses and coats made up in various colours, fabrics and sizes, to be sold in Paris department stores and in selected shops elsewhere. Usually, even in the mass-produced versions, the Worth label was stitched into every garment, so that every *prêt à porter* buyer would feel as if they were just a little bit *haute*

---

[99] Charles Worth's Chambre Syndicale lives on today, as the Fédération de la Haute Couture et de la Mode, the body that organizes Paris Fashion Week and forces French *haute couture* houses to run a Paris creative studio with at least 15 employees, and to present two collections of handcrafted garments per year. *Haute couture*'s protectionism has become even more stringent.

couture parisienne. Which is precisely the impression sold to any tourist today who buys a Dior T-shirt.

However, apparently there were exceptions to the labelling rule, as Jean-Philippe reveals in *A Century of Fashion*: when talking about Princess Alexandra's visit to La Maison Worth in 1878, he says that she only ever ordered two dresses from Worth because 'she was loyal to England and would buy only from British modistes.' However, he adds, 'as these [British modistes] stocked our models for retail purposes, Alexandra wore many a Worth model unawares.'

According to Jean-Philippe, the ultra-patriotic Queen Victoria fell into the same trap. During La Maison Worth's existence, she never bought anything made outside of England, he says. 'Nevertheless, in spite of her rabid allegiance to goods of British manufacture, we made many a dress to her measurements, sold it to her through English dressmakers and had the joy of watching her complacently wear it, believing it untainted by alien handiwork.'

This suggests that either La Maison Worth supplied some dresses without labels, or that at least one canny London retailer removed the labels when trying to sell to the royal family. Unless, of course, Alexandra and Victoria were in reality accomplices in the deception, and were so desperate to wear real Worth gowns that they were willing to compromise their patriotism for the sake of fashion. Royal families have deceived their subjects in much more damaging ways than that.

At this time, Charles also invented a Worth franchise of sorts. He had pattern books printed and sent them twice annually (containing his *prêt à porter* spring-summer and autumn-winter collections) to dressmakers who had signed a contract to buy the necessary fabrics from him. These dressmakers were accredited to manufacture Worth models from his official pattern book.

Charles added an even more competitive gimmick. For years, he had been applying streamlined production techniques, making patterns for stock shapes of sleeve, bodice, etc, that could be adapted for each individual *haute couture* client, with fresh fabrics and trimmings making the difference between creations. This was especially practical if a ballgown had to be made at top speed, because the dress could be assembled from standard parts. It was a process made even simpler by sewing machines, which Charles had begun to use as soon as they were being mass-produced. Carried out by a skilled seamstress, machine stitching could be as good as most work done by hand.

As early as the mid-1860s, Charles had been selling *haute couture* gowns with interchangeable parts. For example, a long-sleeved, high-necked day bodice could be exchanged by a seamstress for a low-necked, lace-trimmed evening bodice – the same Worth gown with two different functions. Now, in his *prêt à porter* range, he went further, and women could buy several sets of different sleeves, as well as lengths of ribbons and lace that could be sewn on if desired. In other words, the customer could revamp any dress to make it look like a new garment, either for a change later in the season or to transform an evening gown into ordinary daywear, or vice versa. Worth dresses as kits – it was a startlingly modern idea, like selling a camera with different lenses.

In Charles Worth's case, these steps towards industrialization could perhaps be interpreted as the aging artist taking a step back from the creative process, allowing garments to be produced 'in his style'. It was a little like Andy Warhol moving from individual oil paintings to multiple prints. But then Charles had always used assistant designers to cope with massive demand, and had often issued instructions as to what fabrics and styles were right for a customer, before leaving his team to create the appropriate dress.

Some might say Charles was cashing in on his name with his *prêt à porter*, but then that was exactly how he had made his fortune – literally making a name for himself, creating *'l'époque de Worth'*. Conscious of the need for dynastic continuity, in 1874 he brought his sons into the family business: 21-year-old Gaston Worth began working on the management side, and Jean-Philippe Worth, who had studied art with Corot, was taken on as an apprentice designer.

Perhaps inspired by the big stores, Charles also added new departments to his range of products. In May 1879 Edmond de Goncourt was surprised to notice an innovation: 'Amongst the young models in Worth's salons who exhibit and parade the celebrated designer's costumes on their slim bodies, there is one young woman, or rather a lady model, whose speciality is to represent pregnancy.' Worth was now designing maternity clothes. He also started making ladies' sports-wear – costumes for riding and boating – and mourning attire. Wedding dresses had long been in the catalogue.

La Maison Worth now dressed women for all occasions. Whether you were a wealthy *haute couture* customer, or could only afford *prêt à porter*, there was no reason to buy any other brand.

19 FINAL ADJUSTMENTS

The *haute couture* business was in no way neglected during Worth's expansion into *prêt à porter*. It was, if anything, growing as fast as before the Franco-Prussian War. As the number of millionaires in newly industrialized Europe and America increased, so did demand for luxury goods, including fashion.

With Gaston's help, Charles re-organized the pricing process, in a touchingly personal way. To ensure that all the company's fitters were working to the same price scale, and to avoid bandying numbers around in front of sensitive customers, they conceived a ten-word phrase – *Chers Frères Worth, on gagne Dieu mais avec volonté – réflechissez* (which could be loosely translated as: 'Dear Worth Brothers, one earns God's love but with determination – consider this.')

The first letter of each word in the phrase was assigned a number starting at 1 for C and 2 for F, 3 for W, etc. and ending with 9 for V and 0 for R. As a tribute to the company's founding father, the first three letters, CFW, stood for Charles Frederick Worth.

Using this system, garments could be priced in code: on an order, lace might be costed as FWR (230 francs), sewing as CRRR (1,000 francs), etc[100]. The rich lady need never be troubled by the reality of finance. The actual figures were sent to the man who, by law, held the purse strings. It was like the sexist custom in expensive restaurants of giving menus with prices to the male diner.

ഗഗഗ

Even if Charles's responsibilities had grown in proportion to the scale of his business, he did not let his natural sense of taste slip at all. And despite his sons' presence, he kept a firm grip on the creative side. His dresses from this period are as stylish as ever. He wholeheartedly embraced and developed the bustle, that cushion-like protuberance over the buttocks that helped to make the waist look slim but made dresses heavy. He is credited with inventing the fan train – consisting of three pleats in the material that began on the bustle and then fanned out behind the wearer, creating a wide train on the floor as she walked.

Charles Worth's outfits throughout 1870s were as architectural as they had been during the crinoline craze, and were designed to use as much fabric as possible. Meanwhile, he carried on squeezing women into rib-crushing tops – so he was still acting as an aesthete and a salesman rather than a liberator of the female form.

He kept as many of his old Second Empire clients as possible, including the exiled Eugénie, who could of course no longer summon him for a fitting. She was now widowed, so her choice of colours was limited by social norms. She spent much of her time in black, grey or pale

---

[100] This pricing process is more fully described in Diana de Marly's 1980 book *Worth, Father of Haute Couture*.

lavender. She attended hardly any social occasions and decided to give away many of the dresses that had been saved from the Tuileries and shipped over to England, some of them unworn.

From her new home in England, she ordered dresses that Charles designed using the measurements he had on record. (Eugénie presumably had seamstresses who could make adjustments to allow for a certain graceful aging). Charles also began sending the Empress an annual bouquet of Parma violets, tied in a mauve ribbon with his name embroidered in gold thread (yes, even his gifts were branded.)

Charles and Marie's fond memories of Eugénie and the Second Empire became even more bittersweet in the early summer of 1879 when they received news that Eugénie's only child, Louis-Napoléon, the so-called Prince Impérial, had been killed at the age of 23 while on an ill-advised mission with the British army in South Africa.[101]

Pauline von Metternich, herself a faithful friend to Eugénie, was touched by this loyalty to the deposed Empress.

In her memoirs, she remarked that: 'He [Charles] was very much attached to the Empress, and, after the downfall of the Empire, he made no secret of his sympathy with the Imperial regime. A fine example to those fair-weather friends who found it easier to forget than to remember the countless benefits showered upon themselves and their relations by the Emperor when he was in power.'

---

[101] For a fuller account of how the British inadvertently contributed to ending the Bonaparte dynasty, see my book *1000 Years of Annoying the French*.

As the burgeoning profits of the 1870s carried over into the 1880s, Charles spent a lot of the cash expanding and improving the château in Suresnes, including having the relics of the Palais des Tuileries erected in the gardens, as we saw in chapter 12.

In 1882, the French government decided that it would be too expensive to restore the Palace. Baron Haussmann and others had put forward renovation projects, saying that it was possible to save the palace. But the idea provoked staunch political opposition amongst republicans like Léon Gambetta: the word 'restoration' had unfortunate monarchist connotations, and rebuilding Napoléon III's old home seemed too reverent to the imperial past. It was therefore decided that the site would be cleared. A demolition company bought the ruins at auction – for 33,500 francs, not much more than the price of one of Worth's most expensive outfits in his heyday – with the intention of selling on relics to collectors.

It was very fashionable at the time to improve one's château or country house with architectural salvage. The Palais des Tuileries was originally built for Catherine de Medici (the wife of French King Henri II) in the 1560s, and had been extended ever since, so many of the pieces of marble lying about were Renaissance and Classical masterpieces.

Charles visited the palace to see what was for sale. We are not sure if Marie went with him on this occasion, but they had certainly walked and ridden past the blackened ruins on many occasions since the blaze eight years earlier. They must have been surprised that the shell of the palace had been allowed to stand untouched for so long. After all, in 1878, the rest of Paris had been spruced up for that year's *Exposition Universelle*.

In 1882, most of the palace was still standing, though it was a roofless, windowless symbol of the end of an Empire. Inside, rubble littered the floors, and there were few if any ceilings. The walls were scorched and pitted with holes from the explosions. Marble fireplaces were covered in ash and dust. Poignantly, some alcoves had survived with their statues intact. The stone staircase Charles knew so well, the one leading to Eugénie's private apartments, was still there, though it had lost its balustrades.

Charles bought more than 20 columns, a dozen pieces of sculpture, and a section of the façade with its balcony and empty window frames, and began shipping wagonloads of stone out to Suresnes. He then designed the Pompeii-like shrine described in chapter 12, and scattered statues around the grounds, including the marble lion sitting by its water feature. By the time the Palais des Tuileries itself was finally flattened in the autumn of 1883, Charles had turned his garden into a memorial to the lost Empire.

ღღღ

Meanwhile, the Worths moved their Paris home out of 7 rue de la Paix, where they needed every square metre for workspace. They had now taken over the whole building, and could easily have afforded to buy it – according to Jean-Philippe, the owners offered several times to sell, but Charles always refused, out of a superstitious fear that changing the lease might change his luck.

Charles and Marie moved in at number one, rue de Berri, on a corner of the Champs-Elysées[102]. This was a

---

[102] Perhaps appropriately, the ground floor of the building is currently a Louis Vuitton showroom.

decidedly chic – and Bonapartist – address. Napoléon III's cousin Napoléon-Jérôme lived at number two. Mathilde Bonaparte moved in at number 20 in 1871 and held her *salons* there. In winter, when it was too cold or wet to ride out to Suresnes, Charles could make the short trip from the rue de la Paix and spend an evening with Marie at the heart of the old-school high society where they had felt most at home.

ʊʊʊ

It was around this time that Charles adopted the highly personal outfit that made him instantly recognizable to anyone who caught sight of him.

As the daily newspaper *Le Gaulois* would describe it in his obituary: 'In his later years, one saw Worth every day, overseeing and directing everything. Dressed in a long cloak of loose woolen cloth, a sort of dressing gown, like one sees in 18th-century paintings; his bald head covered by a wide beret of black velvet, his fingers loaded with jewellery.' It was a *grand artiste* look that would be made famous by the photographer Félix Nadar in his 1892 portrait of Charles.

In fact, the outfit was more 17th than 18th century. The English dressmaker was deliberately adopting the look of the Dutch painter with whom he most identified, Rembrandt, believing that they had both risen to the pinnacle of their craft through pure endeavour, and that they had brought art to the people by selling their work direct to the public (a slightly ironic stance given Charles's reliance on the luxury business.)

In any case, the Rembrandt costume was an unmistakable statement on Charles's part when he sat for Nadar, the photographer who had already published the best-known portraits of the poet Charles Baudelaire and the actress Sarah Bernhardt. The cloak and beret announced to the world that although Worth was head of one of France's most valuable business empires, he was first and foremost a creative genius, and this was how he wanted to be remembered.

The great portrait painters of the day were still enshrining his dresses in art history. As we saw earlier, Winterhalter had been depicting Europe's greatest ladies in Worth creations since the Second Empire. The most fashionable portraitist of the 1880s, the American John Singer Sargent, did the same. As the Tate Britain's 2024 exhibition *Sargent and Fashion* showed, Sargent painted many high-society women in Worth dresses, including Jane Morgan (the wife of J.P. Junior), Margaret Stuyvesant White and Lady Sybil Sassoon. And it was a two-way arrangement: Sargent loved to transfer the dressmaker's elegant fabrics to canvas and his sitters knew that they would look at their most glamorous (and richest) in a Worth gown.

ῶῶῶ

As the 19th century drew to an end, the French Republic became relatively stable. It is true that there were political crises after MacMahon's attempt to restore the monarchy. There was a failed coup d'état in 1889 by an anti-republican former Minister of War, Georges Boulanger; and in 1894 an anarchist assassinated President Sadi Carnot. But there would be no more actual revolutions after 1871, so there was little to discourage rich foreign tourists from visiting Paris.

However, according to Jean-Philippe Worth, French high society had become completely uninteresting: 'After

MacMahon [whose regime ended in 1879] society suffered a total eclipse. Then began an inelegant, bourgeois period in which the receptions and balls were dull, stupid and wholly without distinction.' After the death of Sadi Carnot, he says, came 'the swan song of the last remaining trace of social brilliance.'

In fact, though, Paris's brilliance had simply moved elsewhere, out of the palaces and into the theatres and streets. The *Belle Époque* was in full swing and Montmartre, Pigalle and the boulevards were at their glittering best. Can-can dancers, actresses and *cocottes* (the notorious Parisian call girls) were getting as rich as the *aristos*, and all of them were ordering their dresses from La Maison Worth. Paris was still the world capital of glamour, and French fashions were considered the most desirable in Europe.

This Parisian domination is demonstrated by a series of richly-coloured illustrations in the Victoria & Albert Museum. They are from a British monthly magazine, the *Young Ladies' Journal,* and depict the newest Paris fashions between 1875 and the late 1880s. The magazine printed a monthly supplement which gave readers a detailed description of each dress, as well as the opportunity to buy cut-out patterns.

One of the plates, from the February 1887 edition, shows detailed drawings of 24 gowns, all with bulging bustles and tight waists. These aren't Worth creations, but they prove that Paris fashions were being heavily marketed towards the young ladies of London, and we know that Worth was still the Parisian market leader.

Keeping his hand firmly on the tiller, Charles let Gaston and Jean-Philippe take some of the strain. His health was failing – the migraines that had always bothered him would return at any sign of too much stress. In his diary, Edmond de Goncourt noted that Charles 'comes home in the evening [...] unable to eat, unable to enjoy his scintillating house, suffering from a migraine because of the scents and odours of the grand ladies he dresses all day.'

Marie was now fully retired, a stay-at-home society hostess. There were frequent family get-togethers in Suresnes or at the rue de Berri. Gaston and his wife came to see Charles and Marie every Saturday, and the grandchildren would receive one franc each as pocket money – but only if they were quiet and well-behaved.

ϖϖϖ

Despite his immense workload, Charles occasionally took time off from the business. It has been said by past biographers that he was too busy to return to England before the 1880s, but this is incorrect. According to Rex Needle, a writer and historian based in Bourne, Charles made frequent trips back to his home town to visit friends and relatives, sometimes accompanied by Marie and their sons. For example, after Charles's death an English cousin, Arthur Dean, wrote to Marie to offer his condolences, saying, 'I was only young when you and he last were at Dowsby [the Deans' house in Lincolnshire] years ago, but I have a vivid recollection of seeing you both.'

In his book, *Tales of Bourne in Past Times*, Rex Needle tells an amusing story about one of these visits to Lincolnshire:

> One day, a lady who prided herself on dressing fashionably was waiting for a train on the platform of Bourne railway station

when she became agitated by the conduct of a man who appeared to be keeping her under close scrutiny. Unable to bear such unwanted attention any longer, she sought out the stationmaster and complained that the stranger was rudely walking round her and staring intently at her dress. The stationmaster smiled and replied: "Madam, you should feel honoured, because that man is the great Worth himself."

In 1879, we know that Charles was in London with his son Gaston as a witness in a fraud case at the Old Bailey.

A man called Edward Lawrence Levy was accused (and, partly thanks to Charles and Gaston, convicted) of passing false cheques signed 'C.J. Worth'. On the witness stand, Charles admitted that: 'I do not personally take any part in the financial part of my business,' but assured the judge that he was sure fraud had been committed: 'My initials are C.F. and this signature C.J. Worth on this cheque is not mine.' Levy was sentenced to eighteen months in prison.

In the mid-1880s Charles took a more nostalgic trip back to England, first to the Isle of Wight, which Queen Victoria had turned into a fashionable seaside resort by building a royal residence, Osborne House.

Charles then went inland on a kind of pilgrimage to visit Eugénie, who was exiled in Farnborough, Hampshire, southwest of London. She had just built a large mausoleum for her husband and son, and was living the life of a full-time widow alongside the family vault where she herself would one day be buried.

There, Charles paid homage to his former Empress,

and no doubt they relived the good old days of parties and last-minute alterations at the Tuileries, as well as lamenting Eugénie's personal sufferings.

Soon after this, Eugénie began returning to Paris. Now that the Bonapartes were no longer a political threat, the *République* did not object to her presence.

She would come to stay at the Hôtel Continental[103], across the road from the (cleared) site of the Palais des Tuileries – she was clearly a woman who confronted the past head-on. At the Continental, she received visits from old friends and admirers – like Charles and Marie Worth. It is not thought that she took the short carriage or train ride out to Suresnes. Seeing the chunks of masonry salvaged by Charles might have been one memory too far.

Eugénie continued to visit Paris at regular intervals, often making incognito tours around her favourite haunts, like the vast food market at Les Halles that she had helped to conceive. Her last trip to the capital city that she had once ruled over, both in politics and style, was in December 1919, some seven months before her death in July 1920.

In January 1894, the Worths fulfilled their last order for Pauline von Metternich, who was now well into her fifties and much less of a fashion addict. Her white *moire* (watered silk) dress – costing 2,000 francs, very expensive but a low price compared to her excesses of the 1860s – was sent to Vienna along with a symbol of nostalgic affection for Eugénie, a Parma violet cap (at only 30 francs).

---

[103] Now the Westin Paris Vendôme.

By now Charles and Marie had got into the habit of spending some of the winter months in the south of France – again, following the example of Queen Victoria. They did so in 1894, travelling back up to Paris at the end of February 1895. A few days later, in early March 1895, they received the news that Pauline's husband Richard had died on the first of the month. Another sign that the golden age was over.

On Tuesday March 5, Charles went into work as usual but told his sons that he was feeling unwell, as if a cold was coming on. He had been feverish after going out for a stroll with his grandchildren, and intended to take the following day off.

His sons went to the rue de Berri to visit him on the Wednesday evening, and found him ill in bed, with breathing difficulties. Over the next few days, despite Marie's care, he went rapidly downhill. Charles Frederick Worth died on 10 March 1895, at the age of 69.

ཀཀཀ

The family's announcement of his death gives a full-page list of the bereaved, in order of protocol. Marie is naturally at the top of the roster – named as Madame C.F. Worth – followed by Gaston (the new male head of the family and the firm) and his wife; then came Jean-Philippe (who was unmarried), five grandchildren, and Denis Darcy (Marie's brother-in-law, named as an *'architecte du gouvernement'*). He is named without a wife, because Marie's sister Irma had died in 1884. Then there is a long list of relatives and friends, including the Quinceys, the family of Charles's mother Ann, some of whom called themselves 'de Quincey Quincey', thanks to Charles's uncle Richard who invented the double surname for his son, apparently in an eccentric attempt to be associated with the author Thomas de Quincey.

The announcement ends with a quotation from the Bible, taken from the Book of Ruth, chapter 2, verse 12, which begins: 'Que l'Éternel recompense ce que tu as fait,' or 'The Lord recompense thy work.' Despite the accepted wisdom that you can't take it with you, Marie seems to have hoped that Charles, who had been richly paid for his work in life, was also to be rewarded in the afterlife.

Jean-Philippe Worth described his father's death as 'a bolt of lightning', and said that more than 2,000 people came to pay their last homage to Charles when he was laid out in the drawing room at the rue de Berri.

The funeral took place on 13 March 1895, in the French Protestant church one kilometre or so away, just the other side of the Arc de Triomphe, allowing for a straight procession along the Champs-Élysées and its westward extension, the avenue de la Grande Armée.

The following day, *Le Gaulois* reported that there were more than 1,500 people in the cortege, and that 'a large number of trade unions and commercial syndicates were represented at the funeral by their officials.'

Thirty enormous wreaths were carried on carts behind the hearse, one of which was signed 'One of the wounded of 1870.' The Worths' generosity, turning their home into a hospital for the soldiers who had fought the Prussians, had not been forgotten.

Jean-Philippe wrote that: 'We again had to shake hands with over two thousand more who came to tell us of their sorrow over our loss.' He was so upset that he was 'taken home delirious and given morphine.' He does not record how Marie reacted, after 41 years of marriage and even longer of professional partnership.

Charles was buried in a family vault in the old

cemetery in the centre of Suresnes. Jean-Philippe arranged for a small chapel to be built over the grave, so that Marie would be able go and commune with her departed husband.[104]

ഗഗഗ

The rest of the world remembered Charles fondly. Jean-Philippe said that: 'After the announcement of his death, letters and cablegrams poured in from all corners of the earth [...] They came from kings and queens, from aristocrats and peasants, the bourgeois and the artists and paupers and millionaires.' Eugénie sent a telegram from England that ended, 'In my prosperity and in my sorrows he was always my most faithful and devoted friend.'

The obituary writers were just as eloquent in their celebration of Charles's career.

The Worth family possesses a scrapbook containing some 2,000 or so clippings from all over the western world. Newspapers and magazines in every European capital city – from London to Rome, from Dublin to Stockholm and Moscow – published long tributes, as did practically every small-town local paper right across the USA.

Some of these articles were inevitably reprints of news agency press releases, but many of them were obviously penned by reporters who were passing on a genuinely important piece of world news: The King of Fashion, The Great Man-Milliner, The World's Most Famous Dressmaker was dead …

---

[104] The tomb was destroyed by a German bomb in 1940, and has since been replaced by a plain, flat gravestone.

The Parisian newspapers printed lengthy accounts of Worth's achievements.

In its two-column article entitled 'Le Roi de la Mode' (the king of fashion), *Le Gaulois* opened with an almost obligatory dig at the decadence of the Second Empire and the inflated prices of Worth's clothing, before launching into a brief rundown of Charles's early career that was peppered with factual errors. It is almost as if the hurried journalist (credited anonymously as 'Le Tout Paris' – the whole of Paris) compiled the first few paragraphs from the collective memories of whoever was in the office that morning.

The article alleges that Charles was 'the most Parisian of all Parisians, despite being born American', that he was working at 'la Maison Aurelly' (and not Gagelin) before leaving to start his business at number 5 (sic) rue de la Paix in 1860 (rather than 1858), and that his partner was called Dobergh, instead of Bobergh.

After the disastrous early mistakes, though, the French obituary writer settles into almost pure admiration, and is much more reliable on the subject of Charles's later career: 'It was he who rescued women from the odious and ridiculous crinoline [and] who gradually restored to women's clothing the contours of the feminine form in all its grace and suppleness'; Worth was *'magister elegantiarum'* (the master of elegance), he had 'the dignity of a master' and 'in fashion he created the classical genre, luxurious and of high taste.'

The writer noted Charles's tendency towards snobbery: 'He could have made a grand lady out of a cook, but wanted only grand ladies,' but stresses that 'Worth was as generous as he was extravagant. He donated to every good cause,' and he was always more than fair to his employees, paying 'excellent salaries'.

Le Gaulois acknowledged that Worth was vital to the French economy: 'The domination of French fashions is worth more than 100 million[105] per year to French industry and business. La Maison Worth alone did more than 20 million in business per year, and sent outfits all over the world, as far as Chile, Australia and Japan [...] The name of Worth was known the world over. Being dressed by Worth was a badge of excellence in Chicago as much as Paris, in London as it was in Vienna.'

The reader is left with a moving impression that 'the whole of Paris' was very proud to have been witness to the achievements of this great '*Américain*'.

ღღღ

The paper that Charles read as a young apprentice, the *Illustrated London News*, played a very English patriotic card, announcing that:

> It may be galling to Gallic pride to reflect that not Paris but Lincolnshire produced the Napoleon of dress.
>
> Worth was fortunate to secure the patronage of the Empress Eugénie in the heyday of the Empire, but he ruled that Sovereign as he ruled the American heiresses who became his chief clients.
>
> He was a man of great energy and resource, with a real gift of taste which made it impossible for Paris to teach him anything.

---

[105] The huge sums being quoted become even more surprising when one considers that the average ordinary seamstress in France was still earning only about two francs per day (a little more in Paris).

He was also the greatest minister to feminine vanity the world has ever seen.

On 12 March, *The Times*, the foundation stone of the British establishment, published an obituary in which it apparently apologized to its more old-fashioned readers for stooping to mention lady's clothing, while wholeheartedly praising Charles's success. It called fashion 'a fickle goddess' with 'ludicrous aspects', but:

> M. Worth must have been a man of no common gifts and powers to achieve the distinction in his calling to which he attained. [...] The boy from Lincolnshire beat the French in their own acknowledged sphere. He set the taste and ordained the fashions of Paris, and from Paris extended his undisputed sway over all the civilized and a good deal of the uncivilized world. That was no small feat to perform. Beside the perseverance and the commercial qualities which the establishment and the organization of a great business always demand, it certainly required the possession of genuinely artistic gifts of a special kind.

The writer, clearly a fan, confirms all of Charles's own opinions about his status as a genius:

> M. Worth was a real artist in dress, who took himself and his "creations" seriously [...] No man – no woman certainly – who had seen his or her friends transfigured by Worth *toilettes* has ever failed to pay homage to his inimitable art in "clothing the palpable and

familiar with golden exhalations of the dawn."[106] The experience afforded the spectators a glimpse of a better world, if occasionally it filled their fair bosoms with some of the worst passions of this.[107] For a generation M. Worth has been supreme in his own domain. He has known how to dress woman as nobody else knew how to dress her.

To quote just one of the British local newspapers, on 13 March *The Newcastle Daily Chronicle* wrote that:

> In matters of fashion it is accepted by all Parisians, and most others, that Paris rules France, and that France rules the world. French women are notoriously amongst the least beautiful in Europe, but it is a fact that they have the supreme eye of their nation for effect, and that they know how to walk. In the last generation however, Paris has bowed to the late Charles Worth, and for all that period it is a curious fact that an Englishman should have been the autocrat of Parisian, and therefore of all other, fashions.

On March 16, in a Washington newspaper that the Worth family album does not name, a writer called Kate Field published a personal tribute headed 'A Great Artist

---

[106] A quotation from Samuel Taylor Coleridge's translation of Friedrich Schiller's play *The Death of Wallenstein*.

[107] Perhaps a sop to male *Times* readers who had had to foot dressmakers' bills, or to any Victorian prude who had looked unkindly on low *décolletés* and exposed ankles.

Gone', which opened, 'Worth is dead and I am sorry, for he was original, and original human beings are rare.' She went on to deliver an eloquent account of Worth's innate good taste and his shrewd judgement in dealing with his rich, demanding clients.

At the other end of the eloquence scale, on 23 March a London magazine called *Pick Me Up* printed a poem that starts out: 'Gone is the great dressmaker, Gone to the undertaker,' and goes downhill from there. But even these diabolical verses were presumably intended as a sincere homage to a departed master of his trade.

ღღღ

And so, as the 19th century drew to a close, the world said an overwhelmingly affectionate farewell to Charles Frederick Worth, the man who turned fashion from a handicraft to an industry, the inventor of modern *haute couture*, the first designer to use full-time live models, the creator of the catwalk and the fashion brand, the pioneer of the notion of dressmaker as artist, the stylist who dressed – no, who *created* – the female fashion icons of his day.

He was hailed as a great ambassador of Englishness abroad by the British, and a key player in the French economy by the Parisians. Overall, one of the most famous men of his generation, even of his century.

Just twelve days after Charles's death, Suresnes municipal council debated on whether to name a street after him. At the council meeting, an objector called Monsieur Féron opposed the motion, saying that 'The names of serious events or warriors are preferable.' But he was overruled by a Monsieur Simon who argued that: 'The good acts of this man are of such a great humane nature that they will place his memory above any future variations in public opinion.' As the minutes noted, 'The council unanimously approved these sentiments, minus Monsieur Féron who voted against.' The rue Worth was duly created.

ღღღ

It is only sad that none of Charles's newspaper obituaries mentioned Marie, without whom he may never have created the catwalk, or had the courage to start up his own business, and without whose marketing techniques he might have gone bankrupt in the first year at the rue de la Paix.

In fact, Charles himself was as guilty as any of the obituary writers. In his own account of his career published by the Rochester *Union and Advertiser* on 11 March 1895, just after his death, he does not mention Marie once. The only women he names are the Empress Eugénie, Queen Victoria, Marie-Antionette and Madame de Pourtalès[108].

Incidentally, in this article it is touching to see Charles summing up his career in a way that shows where his true obsessions lay. Almost as an afterthought, he ends his reminiscences with a pithy final paragraph: 'Once I made a dress in whose construction 100 yards of silk were employed.' Extravagant to the end.

Three years later, when Marie succumbed to bronchitis on 8 August, 1898, her professional achievements were ignored, just as they had been on her marriage certificate and in Charles's obituaries.

Le Gaulois announced that 'Madame Worth, widow

---

[108] Marie wasn't the only omission. Pauline von Metternich would certainly have been insulted if she had read the article, as would Charles's most famous American clients.

of the famous dressmaker' had died. It reported that she had 'continued her husband's charitable traditions', that she 'helped people out with perfect discretion' and 'was a good woman in all senses of the word.'

The paper devoted almost as much space to her home as her character, saying that 'the house where Madame Worth died is an immense building, a sort of palace out of *A Thousand and One Nights* where modern comforts are combined with the most refined art.'

Two days later, the same newspaper reported on her funeral, a very grand affair in Suresnes. The crowds came out to pay their tributes and 'the hearse literally disappeared beneath a mountain of flowers, crosses and wreaths.'

One of the wreaths was inscribed 'To Madame Worth, a respectful homage from a wounded man of the 1870-71 war.' The same grateful mourner as three years before?

The hearse was followed through the streets by Gaston and Jean-Philippe, along with the town's firemen, the local musical society, 'numerous important personages from Parisian commerce and industry', the staff of La Maison Worth, as well as 'the entire population of Suresnes, who came to bear final witness to this great benefactor towards simple, humble people.'

We learn that, works by, amongst others, Beethoven and Chopin were performed at the funeral service by singers and musicians from the Opéra de Paris, accompanied by the organist from La Madeleine church. It was a fantastic send-off, but there is no mention at all of Marie's own role in attaining this prominent social position for her family.

To modern eyes, it is all very disappointing. The 19th century was obviously not ready to give recognition to women like Marie – the hard-working wives of the men who held the purse strings – for anything more than their womanly kindness and tasteful homemaking.

EPILOGUE

When Gaston and Jean-Philippe assumed complete control of La Maison Worth after their father's death, the succession was smooth. Jean-Philippe goes even further, saying that the business 'rose like the phoenix from its own ashes.'

Gaston opened a branch in London, so that British *haute couture* clients were not obliged to come to France if they wanted to dress the Parisian way.

Even so, British aristocrats continued to beat a path to the rue de la Paix, where Jean-Philippe took on his father's creative mantle. He had inherited Charles's sense of taste, and continued to design spectacular dresses, reaching the highpoint of his career when the whole of aristocratic Europe needed gowns for the coronation of King Edward VII of England in the summer of 1902.

In his memoirs Jean-Philippe lists his famous customers, including members of Europe's royal families, stars of the stage like the legendary opera singer Nellie Melba, foreign high-society ladies, and the daughters of Charles's clients from elite French dynasties like the Murats and the Mornys.

However, in design terms Jean-Philippe looked mainly to the past, which caused tensions with his more pragmatic elder brother.

Gaston was not a man to rest on his laurels. He even pulled down his parents' sprawling home in Suresnes and built himself a more modest 'villa' (which still looked like a grand hotel). It was more or less a copy of the house that his brother Jean-Philippe had built for himself on the banks of Lake Geneva.

In 1901, Gaston had the good sense to recruit a modern-minded designer, Paul Poiret, who ensured the transition into the 20th century with practical, everyday fashions that Jean-Philippe refused to work on. However, only two years later, Poiret left to found his own fashion house. (Incidentally, he is credited as the first stylist to free women from the tight corset, allowing them to breathe freely at last – usurping Chanel's claim.)

For France and its fashion industry, World War One was a catastrophe far greater than 1870. The focus was naturally on uniforms rather than evening gowns, and 7 rue de la Paix was again turned into a hospital. Gaston's sons Jean-Charles and Jacques both served in the army, and survived, though Jean-Charles received a serious shrapnel wound. But one of Gaston's sons-in-law was taken prisoner and another was killed. Gaston had a nervous breakdown and retired, leaving Jean-Charles to become artistic director and Jacques business manager.

Times were much harder after 1918. The Russian and Austrian imperial families – faithful clients of La Maison Worth – had fallen from power. The whole Russian aristocracy, wildly extravagant buyers of clothes and jewellery, lost their position, money and in some cases their lives. The British and the Americans began socializing again, but there were countless new competitors in the fashion world, and now the Worth brand was just one of many.

The 1920s sounded the death knell of an era for the Worths. Eugénie died in 1920, Pauline von Metternich in 1921, Gaston in 1924, Jean-Philippe in 1926.

In the 1930s, the Worths' land in Suresnes was sold off and cleared, except for Gaston's villa and the original entrance porch, and the site is now home to the local hospital. Some of Charles's souvenirs of the Palais des Tuileries were taken away to the town of Barentin, near Rouen. Others, considered too fragile to move, were copied and then destroyed.

In 1936, the London branch of La Maison Worth was bought out by an English company. In 1950, La Maison Paquin, a fashion house based at number 3 rue de la Paix, acquired the Worth's French *couture* business. The takeover did not bear fruit and the dressmaking side of La Maison Worth closed down in 1956, 98 years after it had been founded.

The company had branched out into perfumes in 1924, with a fragrance called Dans la Nuit, in a bottle designed by René Lalique. When the fashion house closed, the perfumes were sold to the man who had created them for Worth, a perfumier called Maurice Blanchet, and they are still available today. The most famous is probably Je Reviens, which didn't do especially well when it was first launched in 1929, but took off after D-Day 15 years later, when GIs began sending bottles of the perfume home to their loved ones as an optimistic promise of a swift return.

ღღღ

Apart from a brief, nostalgic attempt at reviving the Worth fashion brand in the early 21st century, everything that Charles and Marie created has now died a natural death. After all, their business was a product of a specific period, and it was miraculous that it survived for almost a century.

Even so, the Worth legacy lives on.

First, in some magnificent museum exhibits – plenty of Charles's *haute couture* dresses have been donated to the Victoria & Albert in London, the Metropolitan in New York, the Palais Galliera in Paris and other great collections of historical clothing. They have also been immortalized in portraits by artists like Franz Xaver Winterhalter and John Singer Sargent.

And secondly, in almost every aspect of the modern fashion industry, from the omnipresent brand logos and showroom stores to the look of superiority on the faces of *haute couture* clients in the front row of catwalk shows, and the public personas of the clothes designers themselves who act as though they were Rembrandts.

These big-name designers all claim to invent something brand-new twice a year, but in reality they are simply recycling everything they have inherited, consciously or unconsciously, from Charles and Marie Worth, the inventors of their industry.

SELECTIVE BIBLIOGRAPHY

I consulted so many documents while writing this book, many of them online, many of them single pages from magazines, newspapers and catalogues, that it is pointless listing them all.

The Bibliothèque Nationale's website, *Gallica.fr*, is an invaluable research source with an excellent keyword/date search tool. *Gutenberg.org*, *Archive.org* and the British Newspaper Archive were also very useful.

When excerpts from French texts are quoted, the English translation is my own, except where stated.

Below is a selection of texts quoted in this book (listed by author, title, publisher, date):

Juliette Adam, *Mes Sentiments et nos idées avant 1870*, A. Lemerre, 1905.

F. Adolphus, *Some Memories of Paris*, William Blackwood and Sons, 1895.

Anon, *Attentats et complots contre Napoléon III, histoire complète des attentats et des complots jusqu'à ce jour, accompagnée de portraits et de gravures*, A. Chevalier, 1870.

Maxime Du Camp, *Souvenirs d'un demi-siècle, au temps de Louis-Philippe et de Napoléon III, 1830-1870*, Hachette, 1949.

Amélie Carette, *Souvenirs intimes de la Cour des Tuileries*, P. Ollendorff, 1889-1891.

Jean des Cars, *Eugénie, la dernière impératrice ou Les larmes de la gloire*, Perrin, 1997.

Charles Dickens, *All the Year Round*, Volume IX, Dickens, 1863.

Jules Ferry, *Les Comptes fantastiques de Haussmann*, Guy Durier, 1870.

Valérie Feuillet, *Quelques Années de ma vie*, Calmann-Lévy, 1908.

Gustave Flaubert, *Vie et travaux de R.P. Cruchard et autres inédits*, Presses universitaires de Rouen et du Havre, 2005.

Lillie Hegerman-Lindecrone (aka Mrs Moulton), *In the Courts of Memory, 1858-1875*, Harper & Brothers, 1912.

Lillie Hegerman-Lindecrone (aka Mrs Moulton), *The Sunny Side of Diplomatic Life, 1875-1912*, Harper & Brothers, 1914.

Maurice d'Irisson d'Hérisson, *Journal d'un officier d'ordonnance : juillet 1870-février 1871*, P. Ollendorf, 1885.

Abigail Joseph, *A Wizard of Silks and Tulle, Charles Worth and the Queer Origins of Couture* (article), Victorian Studies, Indian University Press, 2014.

Louise Lacroix (pen name: Marfori), *Biographie d'Eugénie de Montijo, Impératrice des Français*, self-published, 1870.

Diana de Marly, *Worth, Father of Haute Couture*, Elm Tree Books, 1980.

Louise comtesse de Mercy-Argenteau, *The Last Love of an Emperor, Reminiscences of the Comtesse Louise de Mercy-Argenteau, Née Princesse de Caraman-Chimay*, Heinemann, 1926.

Pauline von Metternich, *Éclairs du passé*, Amalthea-Verlag, 1922.

Louis Morin, *Les Cousettes: physiologie des couturières de Paris,* Librairie L. Conquet, 1895.

Eugène Pelletan, *La Nouvelle Babylone – lettres d'un provincial en tournée à Paris,* Pagnerre, 1862.

Henry Du Pré Labouchère, *Diary of the Besieged Resident in Paris,* Hurst and Blackett, 1871.

Georges Renaud, *Prix et salaires à Paris en 1870 et 1872,* Journal de la société statistique de Paris, 1873.

Edith Saunders, *The Age of Worth,* Longmans, Green and Co, 1954.

Albert Dresden Vandam, *An Englishman in Paris,* Smith, Elder & Co, 1892.

Jean-Philippe Worth, *A Century of Fashion,* Little, Brown & Company, 1928.

Émile Zola, *La Curée,* Charpentier, 1871.

ABOUT THE AUTHOR

Stephen Clarke is a Fellow of the Royal Historical Society.

His books have been translated into more than twenty languages.

His non-fiction books include *1,000 Years of Annoying the French* which was a number-one bestseller in the UK, in both hardback and paperback, and was shortlisted for a French history prize, the Prix du Guesclin.

1,000 Years of Annoying the French inspired the permanent collection at a French museum, which Clarke curated. It is the Centre Culturel de l'Entente Cordiale at the Château d'Hardelot in northern France.

He adapted (with French writer Vincent Hazard) an episode from his biography of Edward VII, *Dirty Bertie, an English King Made in France*, into a play for a French national radio station, France Inter.

His best-known novels are the worldwide bestselling *Merde* series, including *A Year in the Merde* (which has sold well over a million copies worldwide) and *Merde Actually* (a number-one bestseller in the UK).

He has written two stage shows based on his books – an adaptation of his novel *The Merde Factor*, and a words-and-music show in French called *L'Entente Cordiale en Paroles et Musique*.

He also writes songs, jokes for stand-up comedians and lyrics for singers, and has co-written a French radio sitcom.

He is a British author living in Paris, where he divides his time between writing and not writing.

CHARLES FREDERICK WORTH

THE ENGLISHMAN WHO INVENTED HAUTE COUTURE

Made in the USA
Middletown, DE
12 September 2025